Everyday Life:

REVOLUTIONARY WAR

WITH CROSS-CURRICULAR ACTIVITIES IN EACH CHAPTER

WALTER A. HAZEN

Good Year Books

Photo Credits
Front and Back Cover Map Background:
Corbis. Front Cover: *t.* SuperStock, Inc.;
b.l. Philadelphia Convention & Visitors
Bureau; *b.r.* Smithsonian Institution.
2: Studio of Allan Ramsay: George III, The
Scottish National Portrait Gallery.
3: *t.* Colonial Williamsburg Foundation;
b. The Metropolitan Museum of Art,
Bequest of Charles Allen Munn, 1924.
(24.90.1566a). 4, 10: Library of Congress.
11: The Granger Collection, New York.
13: Library of Congress. 18: Brown
Brothers. 19: The Granger Collection,
New York. 20, 21: Library of Congress.
26: Print Collection, Miriam and Ira D.
Wallach Division of Art, Prints and
Photographs, The New York Public
Library, Astor, Lenox and Tilden
Foundations. 27, 28: Library of Congress.
29: Philip Gendreau/CORBIS/Bettmann.
34: Library of Congress. 36: *t.* Archive
Photos; *b.* North Wind Picture Archives.
37: CORBIS/Bettmann. 42: Library of
Congress. 43: The Granger Collection,
New York. 44, 45: Library of Congress.
50: David David Gallery,
Philadelphia/SuperStock, Inc.
51: Princeton University Library.
52: Library of Congress. 53: National
Gallery of Art. 58: Electric Boat
Corporation. 59: Hudson Historical
Bureau. 60: Independence National
Historical Park. 61: Courtesy of Heather
Wendt Kemp. 66, 68: North Wind
Picture Archives. 69: The New York
Historical Society. 74: CORBIS/Bettmann.
75: SuperStock, Inc. 77: The Metropolitan
Museum of Art, Gift of William H.
Huntington, 1883. (83.2.1001.). 82: John
Morrell and Company. 83: Library of
Congress. 84: Kevin Fleming/CORBIS.
85: Library of Congress.

Check
out these
other books in
the *Everyday Life*
series from Good Year
Books, including

Dedication
 To Martha, Jordan, and Allison

Acknowledgments
 Grateful acknowledgment to my editor, Laura Strom, who
has guided me through several books in Good Year's *Everyday
Life* series. Without her advice and support, this book would not
have been possible.
 I would also like to thank Roberta Dempsey, Acquisitions
Manager at Good Year, for giving me the opportunity to be a
part of such an exciting project. Her support and confidence in
me is likewise appreciated.

Good Year Books

are available for most basic curriculum subjects plus many
enrichment areas. For more Good Year Books, contact your local
bookseller or educational dealer. For a complete catalog with
information about other Good Year Books, please contact:

Good Year Books
P.O. Box 91858
Tucson, Az 85752-1858
www.goodyearbooks.com

Design and Illustration: Sean O'Neill, Ronan Design
Design Manager: M. Jane Heelan
Editor: Laura Layton Strom
Editorial Manager: Suzanne Beason
Executive Editor: Judith Adams

Printed in the United States of America.

ISBN 0-673-58899-8

 6 7 8 9 - MG - 06 05 04

GOOD YEAR BOOKS

Table of Contents

Table of Contents *continued*

Introduction

On April 19, 1765, the first shots of the American Revolution were fired at Lexington, Massachusetts. On September 17, 1787, the Constitution of the United States was signed at Philadelphia, Pennsylvania. During the 12 years in between, what in time became the United States of America underwent a shaky beginning.

Sometimes the struggle of the American colonies for independence is referred to as the American Revolution. At other times, as in this book, it is called the Revolutionary War. Still other sources favor the War of Independence. By whatever name the revolution is called, it was not some spontaneous event that happened overnight. Quite the contrary. The colonists' revolt against Great Britain came after years of frustration and sincere attempts to work things out with the mother country.

In *Everyday Life: Revolutionary War*, the student learns that the vast majority of colonists never desired a break with Great Britain. Most simply wanted Parliament to repeal acts they considered unfair and harmful to the colonies. Even when matters reached the point of no return, only about a third actually favored war. The remainder either wholeheartedly supported Great Britain or tried to remain neutral.

Everyday Life: Revolutionary War is not a book about battles. Battles, of course, are covered, but the focus of this book is on people and how they reacted and coped with the war and the years immediately following it. The roles of women, children, free African-Americans, and patriotic civilians are given equal space with the soldiers who did the fighting. Stories of individual determination and courage, along with a variety of activities at the end of each chapter, should make the book interesting reading for all students.

Walter A. Hazen

CHAPTER I

The Background

King George III of Great Britain, whose stubborness and lack of insight led England's colonies in America to revolt. From a portrait by Allan Ramsay.

he first shots of the American Revolution were fired in 1775. Yet, in the minds and hearts of the American colonists, the revolution had started 15 years earlier, in 1760. No blood was shed during those intervening years, but many events took place that ended in a war for independence and in the creation of the United States of America.

What happened in 1760 was that Great Britain got a new king. He was George III, a pompous, 22 year old who found himself immediately at odds with his faraway American subjects. His desire to reign rather than rule, as well as his determination to make the colonists help pay the costs of England's Seven Year's War with France, led to conflict from the start.

George III was not the corrupt tyrant that some history books make him out to be. He could, in fact, be rather pleasant at times. But his bouts of pleasantness were overshadowed by his temper and stubbornness. Although Parliament had long ago limited the power of the throne, George III made use of what authority he did have to make life miserable for the colonies.

The problem began in 1763. In that year, the king urged Parliament to pass a proclamation (law) forbidding further settlement beyond the Allegheny Mountains, a part of the Appalachian range. Any settlers already there would have to leave. The proclamation was prompted by a series of Indian raids on settlers in the area. George III reasoned that peace could be maintained with the Indians if colonists were forbidden to settle on Indian land.

The colonists had other ideas. George III was weeks away across a vast ocean and was in no position to prevent his subjects from doing anything. Adventuresome settlers, therefore, continued to pour into the Appalachians in search of better land. By 1770, some 5,000 had ignored the proclamation and moved into the

region. Five years later, Daniel Boone blazed the Wilderness Road through a gap in the mountains and opened the gateway to the great West.

George III was just getting warmed up. In 1764, Parliament passed the Sugar Act. The Sugar Act, which placed a tax on molasses, was the first law designed to raise money in the colonies for the crown. Although the colonists grudgingly paid, the implementation of the tax caused a stir up and down the Atlantic seaboard.

The Sugar Act was followed in 1765 by the Stamp Act. The Stamp Act really raised the ire of the colonists. It required that expensive blue stamps be affixed to all legal documents, marriage licenses, newspapers, diplomas, and a number of other papers. To the people of the colonies, such an act constituted "taxation without representation," and they immediately petitioned the king and Parliament to repeal, or cancel it.

An inscription on a teapot expresses colonial opposition to the Stamp Act of 1765.

All colonial complaints were ignored. In the eyes of George III and Parliament, England was the mother country and the colonists were children whose duty it was to willingly obey. Thus snubbed by the English government, the colonists reacted violently. They attacked stamp sellers both in their shops and on the streets and burned bundles of stamps. They invaded the homes of stamp sellers, gutting their houses and burning their furniture and books. Some mobs even drank the liquor of stamp sellers and uprooted their gardens. No British stamp agents were killed, but a few were tarred and feathered. Melted tar was poured over their bodies and then feathers applied to the tar. The result was a nasty mess that took some doing to get rid of.

While many colonists joined mobs and went about harassing and attacking stamp sellers, others chose less-violent means to express their anger. Some colonists were elected as delegates to a Stamp Act Congress that met in New York. Their purpose was to petition the king, which they did; they were promptly ignored.

A mob gathers around an effigy of a British stamp collector. Stamp collectors were dealt with roughly by irate colonists.

Other colonists took the action that led to the Stamp Act being repealed: a boycott of all English-made goods. When colonists not only refused to buy the required stamps but British products as well, British merchants raised a hue and their cry was heard all the way to London. Faced with such outrage, Parliament repealed the Act in March 1766.

There was joyous celebration throughout the colonies when the Stamp Act was repealed. Happy colonists rang bells, lit bonfires, shot off fireworks, and hosted boisterous parties. They felt they had won a huge victory over the mother country. But George III and Parliament were not to be outdone. Immediately after rescinding (canceling) the Stamp Act, Parliament passed what was called the Declaratory Act. The Declaratory Act stated that Parliament, even though it had just knuckled under to the colonists, had the right to pass any future tax laws as it saw fit.

And it did. The next source of friction between England and the colonies was the Townshend Acts of 1767. These were suggested to Parliament by Lord Charles Townshend, who was the Chancellor of the Exchequer. As Chancellor of the Exchequer, Townshend was Great Britain's finance minister, responsible for collecting revenues to pay for the cost of government. Known as "Champagne Charlie" because of his fondness for the bubbly wine, Townshend urged Parliament to place a tax on such imports as lead, glass, paper, paint, and tea. Revenue collected from the tax would pay the salaries of royal officials in the colonies as well as the cost of maintaining an army so far away from home. (The British colonial army was another thorn in the side of Americans. Two years earlier, Parliament had passed the Quartering Act, which required colonists to house British troops in their homes.)

As with previous taxes, the people of the colonies fought back against the Townshend Acts. Not only did they refuse to buy those British goods included in the acts, but other goods as well. The boycott the colonists started lasted three years and caused much privation in the colonies. But Americans everywhere were determined to hold out. They made do with homespun clothes and

Colonists ready with tar, feathers, and clubs force a merchant to sign a non-importation agreement with England.

substituted coffee for tea. When the acts were finally repealed, the British government left the tax on tea to prove again that it could tax when it well pleased. Such stubbornness on the part of George III and Parliament did little to ease the tension that mounted with each passing year.

Thus far, we have talked only of the immediate causes that led the American colonists to fight Great Britain in a war for independence. As important as Parliament's restrictive acts were in bringing on war, they were not fundamental in nature. The fundamental causes of any war run deeper and go back many years.

The fundamental cause of the Revolutionary War was that the people of the colonies had begun to think of themselves as Americans rather than as British subjects. Separated from England by 3,000 miles of water, settlers who had come to America from all parts of Europe had blended together to form a unique people. Although loyal to the British Crown, these settlers, for the most part, had governed themselves since the first English settlers disembarked at Jamestown in 1603. This is why they reacted so vigorously to Parliamentary legislation that curbed their right to make decisions for themselves.

A Frenchman who settled on a farm in New York state in 1759 wrote a book in which he asked the question: "What is an American?" The Frenchman was Michel Guillaume Jean de Crévecoeur. He changed his named to Hector St. John, but is known in some history books as Hector St. John Crévecoeur.

Crévecoeur described an American as a new kind of individual whose principles and ideas contrasted sharply with the European principles of the day. He pointed out that Americans were proud of their individualism and freedom. They were also proud that they lived in a country where nobility did not exist and one's birth was not a factor in success. They were further proud that they were free to read the newspapers and openly criticize government officials.

Crévecoeur's book was entitled *Letters of an American Farmer*. It was immensely popular and was published in six countries. Not only did it attempt to describe the character of the people who called themselves Americans, it warned the aristocracies of Europe that American ideas of equality were likely to spread across the seas.

The colonists' feeling that they were a new breed of people destined to govern themselves, coupled with efforts to make them pay for the cost of maintaining the colonies, brought them closer each year to war with the mother country.

Name _____ Date _____

Rewrite a Part of History

As you know, Great Britain continued to impose taxes on the American colonies and the colonists continued to resist until an inevitable conflict broke out.

But suppose matters had not turned out that way. Suppose that Great Britain had not only repealed the taxes so objectionable to the colonists, but had granted them representation in Parliament as well. How do you think history might have been different? Would the United States of America have ever come into existence? Write your opinions on the lines to the right.

Everyday Life: Revolutionary War copyright © Good Year Books.

Name _____ Date _____

Name Those Colonies

Place each of the 13 original colonies under the proper column. Then, list the chief products associated with each section.

New England Colonies **Chief Products**

_____ _____
_____ _____
_____ _____
_____ _____

Middle Colonies **Chief Products**

_____ _____
_____ _____
_____ _____
_____ _____

Southern Colonies **Chief Products**

_____ _____
_____ _____
_____ _____
_____ _____

Name _____ Date _____

Create a Dialogue

You will remember that the Proclamation of 1763 forbade further settlement west of the Allegheny Mountains in the Appalachian chain. You will also recall that land-hungry settlers, for the most part, paid the proclamation little heed.

On the lines provided, create a conversation that might have taken place among members of a pioneer family as they contemplate (think about) striking out across the mountains in defiance of the law.

_____

_____

_____

_____

_____

_____

_____

_____

_____

_____

_____

_____

_____

_____

_____

_____

_____

_____

_____

_____

_____

_____

_____

_____

Name _____ Date _____

Distinguish Between Fact and Opinion

Can you tell the difference between a fact and an opinion? Sometimes it is not easy to do. In our daily conversations, we make statements we think are facts but which in reality are opinions. Facts are things that are true and can be proven; opinions are simply strong beliefs.

Here are statements related to the material you read in Chapter One. On the blank line to the left of each, write **F** if you think the statement is a fact. Write **O** if you think it is an opinion.

_____1. Had it not been for the Proclamation of 1763, the Indians would have driven the English colonists into the sea.

_____2. King George III was one of Great Britain's most able rulers.

_____3. The colonists felt that taxation without representation was unfair.

_____4. Daniel Boone blazed a trail through the mountains that opened up the way to the West.

_____5. Great Britain saw the American colonies as children whose duty it was to obey the mother country.

_____6. All Englishmen in Great Britain viewed the colonists as upstarts who should be dealt with severely.

_____7. Everyone in the colonies hated King George III.

_____8. Parliament was justified in passing the Declaratory Act after the Stamp Act was appealed.

_____9. All colonists supported the boycott of English goods that followed the passage of the Townshend Acts.

_____10. The colonists' boycott of English goods succeeded in getting the Townshend Acts repealed.

_____11. By the 1760s, the people who had settled along the Atlantic Seaboard had begun to think of themselves as Americans.

CHAPTER 2

Colonial Resistance Grows

To look at Samuel Adams, one would never have guessed that he was a "rabble rouser" and the leading spokesman for American independence. In appearance, Adams was pudgy and rumpled, looking more like a colonial shopkeeper than a revolutionary. But that just goes to show that looks can be deceiving. Adams was a fearless firebrand who for years proved to be a thorn in the side of the British.

Samuel Adams' revolutionary activities began in Boston in 1765. In protest to the Stamp Act passed that year, Adams organized the Sons of Liberty. The Sons of Liberty was a secret organization determined to make life uncomfortable for British authorities. In this endeavor they succeeded. Not only did they harass stamp agents into resigning, they ransacked and burned the homes of several British officials, including the mansion of Governor Thomas Hutchinson. In time, every colony along the Atlantic Seaboard had its own Sons of Liberty group.

Members of the Sons of Liberty pull a statue of King George III from its pedestal. Such acts of resistance increased as colonial resolve stiffened.

Adams' constant criticism of the British led in 1770 to what is called the Boston Massacre. At least that is what the history books call it. In reality, what happened on the night of March 5, 1770, was no massacre at all. It was an unfortunate incident that resulted in tragedy because of the actions of a small group of colonial agitators.

To understand the Boston Massacre, it is necessary to go back to the Quartering Act of 1765. This act required that the colonists provide lodging for British soldiers as well as supply them with such items as fuel, candles, and beer or cider. The act quite naturally was greeted with resentment, and everywhere British soldiers went they were jeered and taunted. Small boys threw rocks and snowballs at them; everyone shouted "Lobsterbacks" (after the color of their red jackets) whenever they appeared.

Tensions reached fever pitch when, on the night of March 5, a British soldier out looking for part-time work to supplement his meager pay was jostled and teased by an unruly crowd. After some pushing and shoving, the

group of some 100 men made their way to the Boston Customs House. There, they began to heckle the lone British sentry standing guard.

What happened next has always been open to question. The colonial version holds that the crowd was further upset because earlier that day a young boy had been whacked with a rifle butt by the very same Customs House guard. Whatever had occurred, the mob began to pelt the sentry with rocks and chunks of ice. After the soldier had been knocked to the ground by a rather large missile, he called for help. Soon he was joined by seven companions and the commander of the guard, a Captain Thomas Preston.

Captain Preston ordered the mob to leave, at the same time instructing his men to load their weapons. But the gathering of rabble-rousers refused to budge. "Let's see you fire, you Lobsterbacks!" they shouted. "We dare you to fire!" The insults and the name-calling grew worse with each passing minute. "Lobsterbacks!", "Bloody Backs!," and a few more names not suitable for print were hurled at the soldiers.

Finally, a shot rang out. Most sources contend that a British soldier thought he heard Captain Preston give the order to fire. Later, at his trial, Preston stated that he never gave such an order. Regardless, muskets rang out and five Bostonians fell. Three died immediately and two others succumbed later. Seven members of the mob lay wounded.

One of the first to fall was Crispus Attucks. Little is known of Attucks except that he was a runaway slave who may have become a seaman. A large man of stout frame, Attucks was the first African-American to die in the cause of liberty. Was he a hero? It all depends on how one views the Boston Massacre. Most Americans considered the seven who died in front of the Customs House martyrs who gave their lives for freedom. Others maintain that Attucks and his companions were troublemakers who got what was coming to them. You can form your own opinion.

Whatever happened in Boston that March night, the colonists made the most of it. Samuel Adams had Paul Revere, a leading member of the Sons of Liberty and a noted silversmith and printer, engrave a picture showing the British soldiers firing point-blank into the crowd in front of the Customs House. Both Adams and Revere knew that that was not what happened, but they also

British troops fire into a colonial mob in what came to be called the "Boston Massacre." The incident only added to the growing tension between the British government and the colonists.

knew the power of propaganda. When colonists read about the incident and saw the picture, their hatred of the British was intensified.

Before proceeding, it is important to mention the courage shown by a Boston lawyer named John Adams. Adams agreed to defend Captain Preston and the soldiers involved in the "massacre." Skillfully presenting the facts as he knew them, Adams won the acquittal of Preston and six of his men. Two soldiers were found guilty of manslaughter and were sentenced to have their thumbs branded. As for Adams, his fear that by taking on the case his career might be ruined never materialized. In 1796, the American people elected him second president of the United States.

After the Boston Massacre, the British withdrew their troops from the city, and things settled down for awhile. But the calm was short-lived. As conflict between Great Britain and the colonists continued, Samuel Adams started what was called Committees of Correspondence in Massachusetts in

Paul Revere, a Boston silversmith and patriot who played a leading role in events leading up to the American Revolution.

1772. Within a year, similar committees were organized in the 12 other colonies. Made up of such respected colonial leaders as Thomas Jefferson and Patrick Henry, the committees wrote letters back and forth, keeping people informed of events. They also saw to it that colonial resentment of British rule remained at fever pitch.

Discounting one or two tax officials who were tarred and feathered, the first act of violence against British authority occurred in 1773. On December 16 of that year, about 100 patriots decided to show King George III and Parliament what they thought of a new tax imposed on tea. Dressed as Mohawk Indians and including in their ranks such well-known personalities as John Hancock and Paul Revere, they boarded three British ships in Boston Harbor and dumped 342 chests of tea into the water. The colonists referred to the caper as the Boston Tea Party. The British had other words for it and would make the colonists pay for their impertinence.

Why the British navy took no steps to stop the "party" is a mystery. There were other British ships only a short distance away in the harbor, and their commander, an Admiral Montague, was spending the night in a house at the end of the very same wharf. The admiral, in fact, is said to have opened his

Everyday Life: Revolutionary War copyright © Good Year Books.

window and shouted something to the effect that, although the "boys" had had an enjoyable evening, they were going to pay for their night of fun.

Bostonians were unmoved by the threat. The next day, they went around singing a song that began:

"Rally, Mohawks! Bring out your axes,
And tell King George we'll pay no more taxes . . ."

The British reaction to the Tea Party was swift. Parliament passed the Boston Port Act, which, on June 1, 1774, closed the port of Boston until the city paid for the tea that was dumped into the harbor. The effect on Bostonians was severe. With the port closed to all commerce, many people were thrown out of work. Worse, no food could enter the city, making the prospect of large-scale starvation a real possibility. As further punishment for the upstart patriots, Parliament increased the power of the royal governor while at the same time decreasing that of the Massachusetts legislature.

The Boston Tea Party, in which colonists disguised as Mohawk Indians boarded British ships and dumped several hundred chests of tea into Boston Harbor. From an 1848 Curriers print.

The Boston Port Act was the first of a number of laws referred to as the Intolerable or Coercive Acts. They included, among others, a stronger Quartering Act and a law empowering officials to send colonists accused of crimes against the Crown across the ocean to England for trial. Incensed, the Committees of Correspondence in Massachusetts swung into action. They sent messages to the other colonies, who sent messages of support as well as food in return. On the first day the port of Boston closed, farmers in Connecticut sent a herd of sheep to feed the city's people. Rice arrived from the Carolinas, and even Quebec in Canada sent more than 1,000 bushels of wheat. Money and supplies quickly came in from each of the other colonies.

Thus united, the colonies devised a plan of action. Virginia suggested that each colony send delegates to a convention to meet in Philadelphia in September 1774. At such a convention, the 13 colonies would then decide what steps to take next.

Everyday Life: Revolutionary War copyright © Good Year Books.

Name _____ Date _____

Write the Lead Paragraph for the Philadelphia Pronouncer

News of the Boston Tea Party caused quite a stir when it reached Philadelphia, New York, and other leading colonial cities. At last the colonists were fighting back against the burdensome taxes imposed on them by the British government, and people everywhere were excited.

Pretend you are a roving reporter for the *Philadelphia Pronouncer* and that you were in Boston the night the "party" occurred. Write the lead paragraph to a story describing that momentous event. Be sure to include answers to the five "W" questions: *Who? What? When? Where?* and *Why?* The headlines have been written for you.

The Philadelphia Pronouncer

★ ★ ★ ★ ★ *December 17, 1773* ★ ★ ★ ★ ★

BIG PARTY IN BOSTON
BRITISH TEA DUMPED IN HARBOR

_____
_____
_____
_____
_____
_____
_____
_____
_____
_____
_____
_____
_____
_____
_____
_____
_____

Name _____ Date _____

Solve a Resistance Crossword

Across

1. Samuel
_____

3. Boston
_____ Act

4. _____
Revere

6. Boston
_____ Party

10. Committees of
_____

11. Sons of
_____

12. _____
Massacre.

Down

1. Stamp
_____

2. Boston
Customs
_____

5. Crispus
_____

6. Captain
_____
Preston

7. _____ Hancock

8. Thomas _____

9. Patrick _____

Name _____ Date _____

Dramatize a Historical Event
(A Teacher-directed Activity)

Divide the class into groups and have each choose one of the following skits. Students should use their imagination and creative skills in planning their skit, which should be about five minutes in length.

Students not participating directly in a skit can make simple props and costumes or critique and rate the skits at the conclusion of the activity. There is a lead-in to each skit to help students in their planning.

S k i t 1 — A group of troublemakers surrounding the British sentry in front of the Boston Customs House prior to the occurrence of the Boston Massacre

On March 5, 1770, a British sentry in front of the Customs House in Boston struck a young boy with the butt of his rifle after the lad had taunted him with insulting names for some time. When word of the incident spread, a group of Bostonians quickly made their way to where the soldier was standing duty.

Plan this skit around the confrontation that took place between the mob and the sentry and the dialogue that followed upon the arrival of Captain Preston and additional British soldiers.

S k i t 2 — The trial of Captain Thomas Preston and the British soldiers involved in the Boston Massacre

John Adams, a prominent Boston lawyer, accepted the unpopular task of defending the British soldiers accused in the Boston Massacre.

Plan this skit to incorporate Adams' defense of the accused, including his questioning of key witnesses.

S k i t 3 — Bystanders watching the Boston Tea Party take place on the night of December 16, 1773

The "Mohawk Indians" who boarded three ships in Boston Harbor and dumped expensive chests of tea overboard were not unobserved. On the contrary, thousands of Bostonians stood quietly on the dock and watched as the event unfolded.

In this skit, create a dialogue that might have taken place among persons in the crowd as they watched the Sons of Liberty go about their task.

Everyday Life: Revolutionary War copyright © Good Year Books.

Name _____ Date _____

Write a Letter

To punish the people of Massachusetts for the Boston Tea Party, Parliament passed the Boston Port Act in 1774. This act closed the port of Boston to trade, making it difficult for the residents of the city to obtain food and other necessary supplies. In addition, Thomas Hutchinson was removed as royal governor and replaced by General Thomas Gage.

Imagine you are living in Boston in 1774 and, along with members of your family, you are beginning to feel the effects of the recent act. Write a letter to General Gage imploring him to repeal the act at once.

Date _____

Honorable General Gage,

_____

_____

_____

_____

_____

_____

_____

_____

_____

_____

_____

_____

_____

_____

_____

_____

_____

Sincerely,

_____

CHAPTER 3

The Continental Congresses

The enforcement of the Boston Port Act and other "Intolerable Acts" in 1774 stirred the colonists to action. With Virginia and Massachusetts leading the way, the First Continental Congress assembled at Philadelphia on September 5, 1774. It remained in session until October 26. Upon adjourning, it promised to meet again on May 10, 1775, if Parliament had not addressed the grievances presented to the king by the delegates. It was while the Second Continental Congress was in session that the first shots of the Revolutionary War were fired.

Carpenter's Hall in Philadelphia, where the first Continental Congress met in September–October, 1774.

But first things first. The 56 delegates who made up the First Continental Congress represented every colony except Georgia. Georgia at the time was under the thumb of a strong royal governor and was in no position to openly defy the Crown. The people of Georgia, however, did get word to the Congress that they would support any decision and measures adopted by the delegates.

Included among the 56 delegates at Philadelphia were some of the most influential men in America. Virginia was represented by the likes of George Washington, Patrick Henry, and Thomas Jefferson. From Massachusetts came John and Samuel Adams, while Pennsylvania was ably represented by Benjamin Franklin and John Dickinson. John Jay from New York and John Randolph from South Carolina were other leading figures in attendance.

The delegates who assembled at Philadelphia were a mixture of moderates and radicals. In politics, a moderate is a person who tries to look at both sides of an issue and seeks a peaceful solution to the problem. A radical, on the other hand, favors extreme and sometimes violent means to attain an end. John Dickinson was a leading spokesman for the moderates, while South Carolina's Christopher Gadsden and Virginia's Patrick Henry argued the cause of the radicals. Patrick Henry summed up the view of the radical side when he shouted, "I know not what course others may take, but as for me, give me liberty or give me death!"

Everyday Life: Revolutionary War copyright © Good Year Books.

At the beginning, the majority of the delegates to the Congress had no wish to separate from Great Britain. Most considered themselves loyal British subjects who had been denied the rights and liberties granted to other Englishmen. They did not even seek representation in the Parliament in London, realizing that such a desire would be difficult to attain. What they did demand, however, were the liberties they felt were their just due along with the right to govern themselves.

For a while, the moderates in the First Continental Congress had their way. They adopted a "Declaration of Rights and Grievances" to present to King George III. In their declaration, they asserted that as English subjects they should have the right of self-government. They also asked that all restrictive laws passed by Parliament since the Proclamation of 1763 be repealed. Their declaration was duly presented to the king, who promptly ignored it. "Anyone who does not agree with me is a traitor and a scoundrel" was George III's reply to the defiant American colonists.

When it was clear that the moderates' approach to dealing with Great Britain would get nowhere, the radicals at Philadelphia took the initiative. First, they called for Committees of Inspection to be elected in every town to see that the boycott of English goods was observed. Whereas Americans earlier had merely been asked not to buy English goods, they were now watched to see that they complied.

Another step taken by the more radical delegates of the First Continental Congress was to call on each of the colonies to form militias and begin preparation for war. Perhaps the best known of the organized militia groups were the minutemen of Massachusetts. The name is especially associated with the group of farmers who fired the opening shots of the revolution at Lexington and Concord. It should be pointed out, however, that the minutemen as portrayed in most history texts are a myth. Most minutemen were not crack shots who easily picked off British redcoats from behind fences and trees. In general, they were poor marksmen, and very few of them actually saw battle. The minutemen were in existence only six months, and some individual members held the title of "minuteman" only a few days.

"GIVE ME LIBERTY, OR GIVE ME DEATH !"

Patrick Henry delivering his famous "give me liberty or give me death" speech before the Virginia Provincial Convention.

By the time the Second Continental Congress met on May 10, 1775, the first shots of the Revolutionary War had been fired. How these first skirmishes (fights) between the colonists and the British came about is covered in detail in Chapter 4.

Meanwhile, back at the convention in Philadelphia many of the same delegates who attended the First Continental Congress eight months earlier were again in attendance. They included George Washington, Patrick Henry, Benjamin Franklin, and John and Samuel Adams. Some, such as Patrick Henry, left early to attend to urgent political affairs in their home states.

The delegates at the Second Continental Congress were an interesting lot. There was Richard Henry Lee from Virginia, who kept one of his hands covered with a handkerchief because his fingers had been shot off in a hunting accident. Also from Virginia was Benjamin Harrison, whose son and great-grandson would become presidents of the United States. Harrison had the distinction of being the largest man at the convention, standing 6 feet 4 inches tall and tipping the scales at 400 pounds. (Excessive weight seemed to characterize many of the delegates. John Adams from Massachusetts, who stood only 5 feet 6, weighed 275 pounds. Such girth was the result of colonials eating meals that sometimes consisted of nine or more courses.)

John Hancock defiantly signs his name to the Declaration of Independence in huge letters for the benefit of King George III. From a Currier & Ives print.

A look at the Declaration of Independence that all of the delegates later

signed points to even more interesting facts about the men of the Second Continental Congress. As you will notice, the signature of John Hancock dwarfs the others on the historic document. Hancock later explained that he wrote his name in extremely large letters so that King George III would have no trouble reading it.

Another signature that stands out was obviously written by someone with a trembling hand. Stephen Hopkins of Rhode Island suffered from palsy, a form of paralysis. As a result, his signature was barely legible. Hopkins said after signing the declaration, "My hands tremble, but my heart does not." Finally, one sees the signature of Button Gwinnett of Georgia. Gwinnett arguably had the most unusual name of any of the delegates. He also led a most unusual life, being killed in 1777 in a duel with a rival for the post of commanding general of the revolutionary troops from Georgia.

Everyday Life: Revolutionary War copyright © Good Year Books.

Inasmuch as the men who fired the earlier shots at Lexington and Concord were militiamen and not regular troops, one of the first steps taken by the Second Continental Congress was the creation of the Continental Army in June 1775. A second important step was to find an able person to command it. When John Adams stood up in the Congress and said he was prepared to nominate the most qualified person in attendance, delegate John Hancock from Massachusetts beamed. Hancock from the start had considered himself the best choice for the position. Besides, it was his money that was paying for much of the Congress' expenses. That alone should carry some weight, he reasoned.

Second Continental Congress

But John Adams did not nominate John Hancock to lead the army. Instead, he proposed that George Washington accept the generalship. Adams' nomination was a blow to Hancock's pride, but Washington was by far the best choice. He had served well in the French and Indian War, and he was a man of great character and determination. People everywhere had confidence in this tall, powerful 43-year-old Virginian to turn raw recruits into a respectable army.

At the same time that Washington was named commander of the army, the Second Continental Congress also appointed four major generals. They were Israel Putnam of Connecticut, Artemis Ward of Massachusetts, Philip Schuyler of New York, and Charles Lee of Virginia. This done, Washington immediately left Philadelphia for Cambridge, Massachusetts, to take command of the volunteer soldiers who had gathered there.

Even though Washington was on his way to form an army, and shots had already been fired at Lexington and Concord in Massachusetts, the Second Continental Congress made one last attempt to work things out with Great Britain. They sent a final letter to the king, a proposal that was called the Olive Branch Petition. (An olive branch is a symbol of peace.) George III stubbornly refused to even look at it.

The die was cast. This meant that the die (dice) had been rolled and there was now no turning back.

Name _____ Date _____

Name Those Notable People

Listed here are the names of ten important persons who were discussed in Chapter 3. Use their names to fill in the blanks in front of the statements that appear below the name box.

Button Gwinnett	Philip Schuyler
Stephen Hopkins	Patrick Henry
George Washington	Richard Henry Lee
King George III	Benjamin Harrison
Israel Putnam	John Hancock

_____ 1. I said, ". . . give me liberty or give me death."

_____ 2. I was a major general from New York.

_____ 3. I lost three fingers in a hunting accident.

_____ 4. After signing the Declaration of Independence, I said, "My hands tremble, but my heart does not."

_____ 5. I was killed in a duel in 1777.

_____ 6. I was disappointed when I was not appointed commander of the Continental Army.

_____ 7. I was a major general from Connecticut.

_____ 8. I said, "Anyone who does not agree with me is a traitor and a scoundrel."

_____ 9. I was appointed commander of the Continental Army.

_____ 10. I was the largest delegate at the Second Continental Congress.

Everyday Life: Revolutionary War copyright © Good Year Books.

Name _____ Date _____

Solve Some Convention Math Problems

ere are several word problems having to do with the Second Continental Congress. Solve each in the space provided, and write the correct answer on the appropriate line.

1. The ages of seven of the delegates to the Second Continental Congress were as follows:

Delegate	Age
George Washington	43
Patrick Henry	39
Benjamin Franklin	69
Thomas Jefferson	32
John Adams	40
John Hancock	38
John Dickinson	43

a. Which age represents the median? _____ The mean (rounded)? _____

b. What is the mode? _____ The range? _____

2. The First Continental Congress opened on September 5, 1774. It adjourned on October 26, 1774. How long was it in session?

_____ weeks and _____ days

3. A delegate to the Second Continental Congress rode his horse from Harrisburg, Pennsylvania to Philadelphia, a distance of about 100 miles. He stopped along way four times for rest periods of 30 minutes each. If his horse averaged 10 miles per hour at the gallop, how many hours did it take him to reach Philadelphia?

_____ hours

Everyday Life: Revolutionary War copyright © Good Year Books.

Name _____ Date _____

Test Your Knowledge of Pennsylvania

Pennsylvania was located in the middle of the 13 American colonies. There were six states to its north and six to its south. Because of its central location, Pennsylvania was the state chosen to host both the First and Second Continental Congresses.

How much do you know about Pennsylvania today? Could you locate it on an unlabeled map? Do you know the names of its capital and other principal cities? Do you know which states border it?

Here are some questions about Pennsylvania. See how many you can answer on your own. If you need help, refer to an atlas or an encyclopedia.

1. What is the capital of Pennsylvania? _____

2. Who founded Pennsylvania in 1681? _____

3. What does the name *Pennsylvania* mean? _____

4. On which of the Great Lakes does the northwestern corner of Pennsylvania border? _____

5. Pennsylvania's largest city is _____.

6. Pennsylvania's second largest city is _____.

7. Which religious group in Pennsylvania still relies on horses and buggies for transportation and refuses to avail themselves of both electricity and telephones? _____.

8. Which state lies to the north of Pennsylvania? _____

9. Pennsylvania is bordered on the east by the states of _____ and _____.

10. To the west of Pennsylvania is the state of _____.

11. Four states border Pennsylvania to the south. They are _____, _____, _____, and _____.

12. The names of two major league baseball teams in Pennsylvania are the _____ and the _____.

13. The names of two NFL professional football teams in Pennsylvania are the _____ and the _____.

Everyday Life: Revolutionary War copyright © Good Year Books.

Name _____ Date _____

Draft a Petition to the King

Imagine you are a delegate to the First Continental Congress in Philadelphia. Also imagine that you have been asked to draft (write or draw up) a petition to King George III in which you list the grievances of the colonies against the Crown.

What would you include in your list? Think of all the ways in which the colonists considered themselves unfairly treated and include them in your petition.

Date _____

His Majesty, King George III:

_____

_____

_____

_____

_____

_____

_____

_____

_____

_____

_____

_____

_____

_____

Sincerely,

_____

CHAPTER 4

The Opening Shots

Who fired that famous "shot heard 'round the world" that history books love to talk about: the shot at Lexington that started the American Revolution? No one knows for certain; each side afterwards blamed the other. But it really didn't matter. When those opening rounds were fired before dawn on April 19, 1775, the colonists were committed to a fight for independence. There was no turning back; the revolution had begun.

The encounter that morning at Lexington, Massachusetts, stemmed from the British goal of seizing a cache (store) of weapons and ammunition that the Americans had accumulated at Concord, some eighteen miles from Boston. The task fell to General Thomas Gage, who was also the royal governor of Massachusetts. Now General Gage was not a bad sort. In fact, he had an American wife. But as a British soldier and royal governor, it was his duty to send troops to Concord to take possession of the weapons.

When the Americans got word of Gage's intentions, they reacted immediately. Three riders, Paul Revere, William Dawes, and Samuel Prescott were sent by different routes to warn the people of Concord. Paul Revere was also concerned about John Hancock and Samuel Adams, who were hiding in Lexington, which was on the route to Concord. The troops dispatched by General Gage had orders to arrest Hancock and Adams, both of whom had proved to be a thorn in the side of the Crown.

There were two ways the British could reach Concord from Boston. One was to go overland; the other was to cross the Charles River to Charleston and then proceed by land. To know for sure which route the British would take, Paul Revere arranged for a friend to set two signal lanterns in the steeple of the Old North Church in Boston. If his lookout friend saw the British board boats to cross the river to Charleston, he would light both lanterns. If he saw them depart by land, he would light one. As it turned out, the British took the water route to Charleston and then continued on by land.

American militia fire on British troops at the North Bridge during the Battle of Concord.

At approximately 4:30 on the morning of April 19, 1775, the British reached Lexington. There they were met by some 70 militia under the command of Captain Jonas Parker. Captain Parker must have been discouraged, for earlier that morning twice that number had responded to the toll of the bell calling them to the village green. But after waiting around for hours, many had grown weary and returned to their homes. Thus, Captain Parker was left with half the local militia to confront some 600 crack (well-drilled) British troops.

The British approached the village green, led by Major John Pitcairn. Calling the Americans rebels and warning them that they would soon be "dead men," he ordered them to lay down their arms. At some point, a shot rang out. Whether it was fired by a trigger-happy militiaman or a trigger-happy British soldier has always been open to dispute. At all events, a British volley killed Captain Parker and seven (some sources say eight) of his men. Nine or ten others lay wounded on the ground.

The Battle of Lexington, where the first shots of the American Revolution were fired on April 19, 1775. From a painting by Alonz Chappel.

As the sun rose, the British marched on to Concord. There they encountered a force composed of over 300 farmers, craftsmen, and shopkeepers from neighboring towns who had heeded the ringing of the bell in Concord and hurried to reinforce the 150 Concord militiamen already there. In the face of such large numbers, the British began to retreat back to Boston.

The retreat along the road to Boston was a nightmare for King George's troops. Trained to fight in tight formation, they were no match for the militiamen who fired from concealment. If you had been a roving reporter at the time and had interviewed a British soldier afterwards, he more than likely would have complained that the Americans cheated and didn't play by the rules. In a sense, they did. Instead of fighting out in the open as was the custom of the time, the sneaky Americans hid behind houses, walls, fences, and barns, and fired at the British as they marched by. Each time the redcoats passed and disappeared from view, the Americans ran alongside them (hidden by the woods), took up new positions ahead, and fired away as they reappeared. Only because the British were reinforced by the arrival of 1,000 additional troops did their entire force escape annihilation. As it turned out,

they suffered 273 casualties on the 18-mile retreat to Boston. The American casualties totaled about half that number.

No sooner had the British arrived back in Boston than they found themselves encircled by 15,000 New England militiamen occupying the surrounding hills. Two of these hills—Bunker and Breed's—afforded excellent vantage points from which to bombard the city below. Consequently, on the night of June 16, 1775, a group of Massachusetts militia under Colonel William Prescott were directed to fortify Bunker, the higher of the hills. But, because Breed's Hill was closer to Boston, Prescott decided to build his main base there and dig in on Bunker Hill later. What all this ultimately meant was that the famous Battle of Bunker Hill, which textbooks rave about, was actually fought on Breed's Hill.

The Battle of Breed's Hill, which took place on June 17, 1775, pitted 1,600 Americans under Colonel Prescott against 2,400 British regulars commanded by General William Howe. From the outset, it appeared that the odds were stacked against Prescott. His men had marched and dug the entire night before, and by dawn they were out of water. Worse than that, they had only about 15 bullets apiece and very little gunpowder. Small wonder that Prescott directed his troops not to fire at the British until they could see the "whites of their eyes."

American and British forces battle it out on Breed's Hill near Boston. Textbooks mistakenly place the battle on Bunker's Hill.

The attack on Breed's Hill began the following morning after the British realized what had happened overnight. Loading into barges, British soldiers began paddling across the Charles River to Charlestown. From their position on Breed's Hill, the Americans could hear British fifes playing and British drums drumming. Surely the sight of such a force frightened the raw American militiamen, who had no training and very few resources to go up against troops of such a powerful European army.

Waiting until the British redcoats were within 15 to 20 paces before firing their muskets, the Americans on Breed's Hill twice threw the attackers back. But on the third try, British General Howe, reinforced by Sir Henry Clinton, succeeded in overrunning the American position. Out of ammunition and reduced to fighting with rifle butts and rocks, Prescott's men withdrew from

Everyday Life: Revolutionary War copyright © Good Year Books.

the hill. Their withdrawal, however, was more of an orderly retreat than a rout, a feat that did not go unnoticed by the victorious British.

The Battle of Bunker (Breed's) Hill proved costly for the British. They suffered 1,054 casualties, a number that included 92 officers. Prescott's troops counted 100 dead, 267 wounded, and 30 captured. Although the engagement was a battlefield victory for the British, it was a moral victory for the

Americans. Prescott's militiamen had proven that they could stand up against a well-trained army and more than hold their own. They were proud that they were forced to retreat only because they ran out of ammunition.

The battles that took place in and around Boston in 1775 were not the only engagements that year. Three weeks after Lexington and Concord, and more than a month prior to Bunker Hill, Ethan Allen and his "Green Mountain Boys" from Vermont seized a valuable prize from the British. On May 10, they stormed Fort Ticonderoga on

Fort Ticonderoga in New York, whose captured guns proved instrumental in causing the British to abandon Boston.

Lake Champlain in upper New York State. Their screaming and yelling, not to mention their rough appearance, caused the British sentry at the gate of the small fort to turn and run. Thus entering uncontested, the Americans caught everyone inside by surprise, including the commander, who came running up holding his pants in his hands and asking what all the commotion was about. Without firing a shot, Allen and the Green Mountain Boys took possession of a British fort.

The purpose of the "attack" on Fort Ticonderoga was to seize the heavy guns the British had there. These included 43 cannons, 14 mortars and coehorns (small mortars for firing grenades), and two howitzers. Seven months after the capture of the fort, a small force under Colonel Henry Knox returned to Ticonderoga to retrieve the guns. With great effort, Knox moved the guns to Boston. The heavy load was first transported by water and then put on sleds and pulled across the snowy countryside. After seven weeks, the guns arrived at Boston, where they were put into place in the hills above the city. The presence of so many fine cannons caused the British to later pull out of Boston.

Everyday Life: Revolutionary War copyright © Good Year Books.

Name _____ Date _____

Conduct an Interview

Imagine yourself a reporter for a London newspaper. You have been sent to America to cover the growing strife between the British government and the colonies. When you learn that British troops are preparing to march on Concord and seize a store of weapons assembled there by the local militia, you arrange for an interview with their commander, General Thomas Gage.

Include in your interview General Gage's thoughts at the moment and what he expects to happen when he reaches his destination.

_____
_____
_____
_____
_____
_____
_____
_____
_____
_____
_____
_____
_____
_____
_____
_____
_____
_____
_____
_____
_____
_____
_____

Name _____ Date _____

Name Those Synonyms and Antonyms

Y ou know that a synonym has the same meaning as another word, whereas an antonym has the opposite meaning.

Here are 20 words taken from the chapter you have just read. On the lines provided, write a synonym and an antonym for each.

	Synonym	Antonym
1. dawn (n)	_____	_____
2. independence	_____	_____
3. concerned	_____	_____
4. proceed	_____	_____
5. depart	_____	_____
6. discouraged	_____	_____
7. responded	_____	_____
8. disappeared	_____	_____
9. excellent	_____	_____
10. outset	_____	_____
11. powerful	_____	_____
12. succeeded	_____	_____
13. costly	_____	_____
14. included	_____	_____
15. proud	_____	_____
16. prior	_____	_____
17. valuable	_____	_____
18. rough (adj)	_____	_____
19. heavy	_____	_____
20. started	_____	_____

Name _____   Date _____

Solve Some Battlefield Math Problems

Solve three word problems, and write the correct answers on the blank lines. Space is provided for you to work each problem.

1. At the Battle of Lexington on April 19, 1775, approximately 70 Americans faced some 600 British troops. What percent of the total number of soldiers engaged were British? (Round your answer.)

_____ percent were British

2. At the Battle of Breed's Hill on June 17, 1775, about 1,600 Americans fought well against 2,400 regular British troops. If the British suffered 44 percent casualties, how many British soldiers were killed, wounded, or missing in action?

_____ soldiers

The American casualty rate was lower, some 25 percent. How many Americans were killed, wounded, or missing in action?

_____ Americans

3. Some sources say that each of the 15,000 New England militiamen who occupied the hills around Boston in April 1775, was supplied with only 36 cartridges. If all 15,000 fired one-fourth of their cartridges at the British, how many cartridges did they fire in all?

_____ cartridges

Name _____ Date _____

Make False Statements True

All of these statements are false. Change the words in italics to make them true. Write the replacement words on the lines following the statements.

1. The first shots of the Revolutionary War were fired while the British were on their way to seize a store of arms the Americans had hidden at *Lexington*. _____

2. On the way to confiscate a store of weapons accumulated by the militia, General Thomas Gage had orders to arrest *Paul Revere* and *William Dawes*. _____

3. *Major John Pitcairn* commanded the American militiamen who encountered the British at Lexington. _____

4. *Fifteen* or *twenty* Americans lost their lives at Lexington.
_____

5. *General William Howe* commanded the 1,600 Americans who fought at Breed's Hill. _____

6. Breed's Hill and Bunker Hill overlooked the city of *Concord*.
_____

7. The Americans defending Breed's Hill retreated after the third British charge because they *were afraid*. _____

8. *William Prescott* led the Green Mountain Boys who captured Fort Ticonderoga on May 10, 1775.
_____

9. Fort Ticonderoga was a British stronghold in upstate *Massachusetts*. _____

10. Fort Ticonderoga was located on Lake *Erie*. _____

11. The British guns captured at Fort Ticonderoga were transported overland with great effort by Colonel *Jonas Parker*. _____

12. The guns from Fort Ticonderoga were instrumental in causing the British to withdraw from the city of *New York*.
_____

CHAPTER 5

The Opposing Sides

A popular misconception held by some people is that most Americans were in favor of breaking away from Great Britain. Nothing could be farther from the truth. When those first shots were fired at Lexington and Concord in April of 1775, roughly one-third of a colonial population of about 2.5 million declared themselves loyal British citizens. Another one-third refused to take sides, preferring to wait and see what turn events would take. That left only one-third in support of open revolt against the British Crown.

Colonists in favor of a break with Great Britain were called *Patriots* (or *Whigs,* after the party in Parliament that generally favored leniency toward the Americans). Those who swore allegiance to King George III and his government were known as *Loyalists* (or *Tories,* after the British party that had no sympathy for the American cause). Those who declared their neutrality on the issue were called *fence-sitters* and worse by both sides.

Relations between Patriots and Loyalists were nasty even before any shots were fired. Loyalists in particular were targets of abuse. One of the first persons to be tarred and feathered in America was John Malcolm, a local customs official in Boston. Resented by the townspeople because he accepted a position from the British, he was dragged from his home on January 25, 1774, and transported by sled to the Customs House. There he was stripped and given a liberal dose of pine tar and goose feathers.

But there was more in store for the unfortunate Mr. Malcolm. Not satisfied with merely tarring and feathering their victim, Malcolm's tormentors further ordered him to curse aloud the royal governor. When he refused, he was given the option of carrying out the order or having his ears cut off. He quite naturally chose the former, after which the mob left him alone. Malcolm spent almost a week in bed nursing his wounds and then sailed for England, where he unsuccessfully sought sympathy from Parliament. Even a piece of skin that had peeled off with the tar, which he took with him as evidence, failed to stir the sympathy of the British.

John Malcolm being tarred and feathered by irate Bostonians. Such was the fate of many loyalists, particularly tax collectors.

Loyalists who escaped being tarred and feathered might be publicly flogged or have their windows smashed. In addition, most colonies adopted laws purposely designed to punish them. Those who openly allied themselves with Great Britain might find their civil rights taken away and their property confiscated. A few of them were even taken out and hanged.

Were the Patriots justified in treating Loyalists so harshly? The Patriots themselves thought so. Loyalists spied and informed for the British army, furnishing them with food and supplies. Thousands more fought alongside the British, either as militia commanded by British officers or as enlistees in the British army and navy. Americans who enlisted in the British military were given five dollars, arms, clothing, and supplies, as well as the promise of land once the upstart patriots were taken care of.

All told, the British government sent about 55,000 soldiers to America to bolster the 4,000 already here. Less than half of these were British, some 30,000 being German *mercenaries* (soldiers for hire who fight for any country that will pay them). To this number was added about 50,000 Loyalists from the 13 colonies, giving the British, not counting their Native American allies, a total force of over 100,000.

As for the Patriots, some 200,000 men enlisted in the Continental Army. General George Washington, however, never had more than 8,000 available for any single battle. At times, his small army stood their ground and fought bravely; at other times they ran away. Short-term enlistments posed another problem for the general. Men signed up for a specified number of months, and, when their time of commitment ended, they simply left and went home.

Discipline in the Continental Army was harsh. It had to be. Soldiers elected their own officers, whom they then often refused to obey. Desertion was a common problem, and more than one mutiny occurred within the Patriot ranks. Both deserters and mutineers were hanged or shot on the spot, and discipline for other offenses was severe. Any troublemaker not confined to the dungeon received a prescribed number of lashes with a whip made of several knotted cords. If the designated punishment called for up to a thousand lashes, these were administered over a period of several days to prevent the accused from dying at the whipping post.

Although most history textbooks scarcely mention it, a number of women and black Americans either served in or accompanied the Continental Army wherever it went. In some regiments, there were often as many wives and children in camp as soldiers. Wives who accompanied their husbands served as

Deborah Sampson, America's first "woman soldier."

cooks, bakers, laundresses, and seamstresses. More than one disguised themselves as men and fought as soldiers.

America's first "woman soldier" was Deborah Sampson of Plympton, Massachusetts. In 1781, just before her twenty-first birthday, she cut her hair and enlisted in the Continental Army as Robert Surtleiff. She fought alongside her male fellow soldiers for almost a year and a half before her true identity was discovered in November 1783. Much to her dismay, she was promptly mustered out of (discharged from) service.

One woman textbooks do mention did not perform the deed for which she is credited. That woman was Mary Ludwig, often referred to as Molly Pitcher. Many sources maintain that Mary continued to fire her husband's cannon when he fell in battle. This is not true. What Mary did was carry pitcher after pitcher of water to the thirsty Continental troops at the Battle of Monmouth in New Jersey. That is how she acquired the name Molly Pitcher.

Ironically, a woman who did actually fire her husband's cannon in battle was Margaret Corbin. When her husband was killed in the attack of Fort Washington in Manhattan in 1776, she took over his cannon and continued to blaze away until she was severely wounded. After the revolution, she became the first woman to receive a pension from the United States government. Why textbooks give credit to Molly Pitcher for something she never did and completely ignore Margaret Corbin is a mystery.

You have already met the first African-American to play a role in the story of America's independence. That was Crispus Attucks, who was killed in the so-called Boston Massacre in 1770. But there were many others. As the war wore on, both sides offered slaves their freedom if they would sign up. Many did. The Continental Army numbered 755 African-Americans by the time the war ended. Prominent among these were Salem Poor and Peter Salem.

Molly Pitcher supposedly firing away at the British at the Battle of Monmouth. In truth, she did not fire the cannon. Molly carried pitchers of water to colonial troops.

Salem Poor was a freedman who enlisted in Massachusetts and distinguished himself at the Battle of Bunker (Breed's) Hill. He fought so bravely that 14 American officers recommended to the Continental Congress that he be rewarded for his conduct in battle. Although he stayed in the army for several years and fought well wherever he went, there is no record that he was ever recognized in any way by Congress.

Peter Salem saw early action at the Battles of Lexington and Concord. He was among the Massachusetts militiamen who forced the British to beat a hasty retreat back to Boston after they failed to find the patriot's supply of arms at Concord. Two months later, along with Salem Poor, he fought at Bunker Hill. He was, in fact, the American soldier who shot and killed Major Pitcairn, who had earlier commanded the British troops at Lexington and Concord.

Peter Salem so impressed his white comrades that they took up a collection and rewarded him for his bravery. After the war, Salem earned a living weaving cane seats for chairs. Seventy years after he died in 1816, the citizens of Leicester, Massachusetts, erected a monument in his honor.

Peter Salem shoots British Major John Pitcairn during the Battle of Lexington. Salem was but one of the numerous free black men who fought with the patriots during the revolution.

In addition to women and African-Americans, the ranks of the Continental Army were swelled by a number of foreign officers who volunteered their services to George Washington. Two of these were the Marquis de Lafayette of France and Baron Friedrich von Steuben of Prussia (later a part of Germany). Lafayette distinguished himself on the battlefield, particularly at Yorktown in 1781. Von Steuben, although equally adept in battle, is remembered mostly for turning Washington's group of rough soldiers into a well-trained, disciplined army.

As mentioned earlier, large numbers of German mercenaries fought for the British. Since most of these came from the German state of Hesse, they were called "Hessians." Of the 30,000-plus who fought in the war, only about half returned to Germany when the fighting ended. Many of those who were not killed stayed on in America as farmers and craftsmen.

Name _____ Date _____

Answer Questions About a Circle Graph

Not counting Native Americans who fought on their side, the British numbered about 105,000 troops in the Revolutionary War. Roughly 80% of these were non-British regulars.

Use the information presented on the graph to answer these questions.

Composition of the British Army

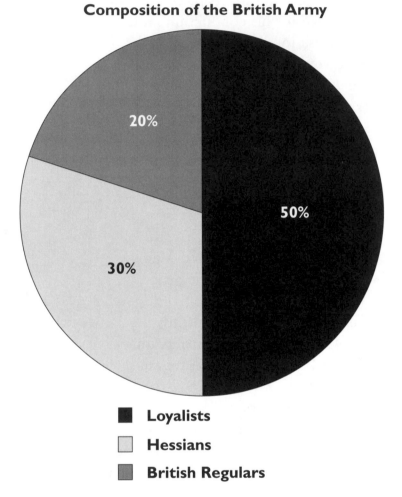

- ■ **Loyalists**
- □ **Hessians**
- ▩ **British Regulars**

1. How many regular British troops fought in America?
   _____

2. What was the number of Hessians who fought for the British? _____

3. There were about _____ loyalists who fought with the British Army.

4. Altogether, about _____ soldiers who fought on the British side were not from Great Britain.

Everyday Life: Revolutionary War copyright © Good Year Books.

Name _____ Date _____

Use Your Critical Thinking Skills

Using the lines provided, write your best answers to these questions.

1. Give reasons why the majority of North American Indians would side with the British in the Revolutionary War.

_____

_____

2. Why do you think half of the Hessian troops who survived the war did not return to Germany when the fighting ended?

_____

_____

3. Many wives accompanied their Continental Army husbands when they left for battle. With this in mind, comment on the next two questions.

 a. If you had been the wife of a soldier, would you have stayed home or gone along with your husband? Why or why not?

_____

_____

b. If you had been a soldier, would you have wanted your wife to accompany you? Why or why not?

_____

_____

4. Should women today be encouraged or even required to fight as combat soldiers? Why or why not?

_____

_____

Name _____ Date _____

Create a Recruiting Poster

In the space given, create and illustrate a poster encouraging Americans to enlist in the Continental Army.

Name _____ Date _____

Use Context Clues to Complete Sentences

Fill in the sentences with the words from the word box.

advancing	dragged	lines
advantages	effective	patriots
allies	factors	rows
announced	familiar	stronger
attack	fighting	tactics
divided	independence	terrain

Americans were _____ in their loyalties when the Revolutionary War began. Roughly one-third supported American _____, one-third chose to remain loyal to Great Britain, and another third _____ their intentions of remaining neutral.

From the start, it would seem that all the _____ lay with the British. The mother country had the most troops, the best weapons, and staunch _____ in the Indians.

On the other hand, the _____ had certain advantages. They were _____ for freedom and independence, both of which are motivating _____ in a revolution. They were also _____ with the _____ on which the fighting would take place. As an added advantage, their supply _____ were considerably shorter than those of the British. Finally, they were quick to make use of guerrilla _____ when they confronted the enemy. The hit-and-run method of _____ used by the patriots was very _____ against the age-old European tradition of troops _____ in neatly-packed _____, as the British were accustomed to doing.

Even though Great Britain was the _____ of the adversaries, the war _____ on for six long years.

CHAPTER 6

The Declaration of Independence

Many people fail at things they try to do or accomplish. Some fail more than once. Ulysses S. Grant, for example, who became a Civil War hero and later president of the United States, failed at both farming and real estate.

Thomas Paine was unique among people considered as "failures." He failed at everything he tried; that is, until he became a successful pamphleteer. He even got an early start at failure. As a young boy in England, he was apprenticed to his father to learn the fine art of corset making. You probably know that corsets were tight-fitting undergarments that women used to wear to make their waists appear smaller. Either Tom never got the knack of making corsets, or he found the task boring, for he ran away to sea when he was 19 years old. And yes, you guessed it: he failed at being a sailor too, and he soon found himself back in England.

Between 1756 and 1774, Thomas Paine tried his hand at a number of trades. He served stints as a collector of excise taxes, a schoolteacher, a tobacconist, and a grocer. As you know by now, he failed at all four. Who knows? He might have failed at more jobs had he not been advised to go to America by Benjamin Franklin, whom he met while the former was in London in 1774.

Thomas Paine had no sooner gotten off the boat in America than he found himself involved in the growing conflict between Great Britain and the colonies. Thanks to a letter of recommendation from Franklin, he got a job as a writer and editor for *Pennsylvania Magazine* in Philadelphia. At long last his string of bad luck came to an end. Paine had found his niche in life: that of a writer.

Thomas Paine may have failed at numerous trades (and even several marriages), but when it came to writing, he had considerable talent. He was so talented, in fact, that a Philadelphia publisher took a financial risk and agreed to publish a 47-page book Paine had written entitled *Common Sense*. That decision on the part of a Mr. R. Bell helped lead to the drafting of the Declaration of Independence.

Common Sense had an immediate impact on Americans. Until 1775, when the book was published, much talk and debate had taken place concerning problems the colonies had

Thomas Paine, whose pamphlet *Common Sense* helped convince the colonies to break with Great Britain.

Everyday Life: Revolutionary War copyright © Good Year Books.

experienced with Great Britain, but no definite plan of action had been put forth. Everyone agreed that something needed to be done, but no one seemed to know just what. The majority of the colonists were not even sure that a break with England was the right thing to do.

Thomas Paine's *Common Sense* changed all of that. Paine listed reasons why a complete break with the mother country was necessary. He cited the British monarchy and how its taxes and restrictions on trade had hurt the colonies. He also stated that it was ridiculous for a country some 3,000 miles across the ocean to rule an entire continent. Finally, he called for the establishment of a republic, where people elect their representatives and do not kowtow to a monarch. "Tis time to part" was the central theme that ran through *Common Sense*.

Americans of all economic classes were moved by Paine's little book. From George Washington and Thomas Jefferson down to small farmers and shopkeepers, Americans began to realize that it was impossible to come to an agreement with Great Britain. Either the colonies had to knuckle under to King George III and Parliament or declare their intention to separate. There is little doubt that Paine's *Common Sense* helped spur the delegates of the Second Continental Congress to write the Declaration of Independence in July 1776.

Benjamin Franklin, Thomas Jefferson, John Adams, Robert Livingston, and Roger Sherman hard at work on the Declaration of Independence.

For 15 months, from the first shots at Lexington and Concord in April 1775, to the drafting (writing) of the Declaration of Independence in July, 1776, colonial troops had fought the British without either a declaration of war or a proclamation of independence. On June 7, 1776, Richard Henry Lee of Virginia presented a resolution to the Second Continental Congress calling for such a proclamation to be drafted.

The delegates to the Second Continental Congress debated Lee's resolution for a few days. Then, because there was some opposition among its members to a complete break with Great Britain, a vote on such a declaration was put off for three weeks. In the meantime, Congress appointed a five-man committee to begin working on a draft that would proclaim America's independence. Included on this committee were Benjamin Franklin, John Adams, and a 33-year-old Virginian named Thomas Jefferson.

Everyday Life: Revolutionary War copyright © Good Year Books.

From the start, the committee turned to Thomas Jefferson to do the actual writing. John Adams told Jefferson, "You can write ten times better than I can," and the other committee members agreed. It was true that Jefferson was an intelligent man. Not only did he write well, he had studied Latin and Greek and had taught himself French, Italian, and Spanish. He also played the violin and would later gain some success as an inventor.

In writing the declaration, Thomas Jefferson was one of the first to call the would-be nation "The United States of America." This name, however, was long in coming. For over a year, people had wrestled with the problem of what to call America, if and when independence came. Some documents and proclamations opted for "United Colonies," while others settled on the unlikely name of "All the English Colonies on this Continent." One of the most frequent names used was "The United Colonies of North America." Information handed out to colonial troops informed them that they were fighting for "The Twelve United English Colonies of North America."

Richard Henry Lee may have been the first to use the word "states" instead of colonies when he presented his resolution to Congress. He stated that "these United Colonies are, and of right ought to be, free and independent States." The new terminology impressed Jefferson and he used it when he drew up the Declaration of Independence.

A copy of the original Declaration of Independence.

The Declaration of Independence is a unique document. It was the first public statement in support of a kind of government never before tried: a government that derived its powers from the consent of the people it governed. Jefferson states at the beginning of the declaration that people are endowed with unalienable rights, rights with which they are born and which cannot be taken away. Among these rights, he maintains, are the rights to life, liberty, and the pursuit of happiness. He continues by saying that it is the duty of the government to protect and recognize these and other rights, and, if it fails to do so, the people have the right to "alter or abolish it." Although such ideas were not new, they were about to be incorporated into a government for the first time in history.

Before Jefferson wrote that people "are endowed by their Creator with certain unalienable rights," he began his sentence by saying: "We hold these truths to be self-evident,

that all men are created equal. . ." This statement has been debated since Jefferson penned it in that summer of 1776. What did he mean by *equal*?

During the 18th century, the terms *men* and *mankind* were used to include both men and women. Was Jefferson doing so when he used the term men? No one knows for sure. It seems obvious that he excluded free blacks and slaves, who at the time made up one-fifth of the population of America. Regardless of the meaning of Jefferson's statement, both women and African-Americans would have to struggle for many years to attain even some of the rights granted to white males from the beginning.

Jefferson finished the Declaration of Independence on June 28, 1776. It was passed by Congress on July 4, 1776 and signed by two men: John Hancock, the president of the Congress, and Charles Thomson, its secretary. Later, when a copy of the Declaration was made on fine parchment, all the members of Congress affixed their signatures.

Signing the Declaration of Independence in 1776. Thomas Jefferson, who wrote the famous document, stands at the center of the table. From John Trumbull's famous painting.

Altogether, 56 men signed the famous document. Included among them were two future presidents, three vice presidents, 10 U.S. congressmen, 19 judges, 16 state governors, and an assortment of other officeholders.

The men who signed the Declaration of Independence knew they were putting their careers and even their lives on line. But they were willing to take that chance to establish a free America. The importance of the moment was not lost on any of them, particularly John Adams of Massachusetts. Adams wrote his wife stating that he believed the anniversary of the signing of the Declaration of Independence would thereafter be celebrated each year with "shows, games, sports, balls, bonfires, and illuminations, from one end of this continent to the other."

How right John Adams was that historic day in 1776.

Name _____ Date _____

Interpret Some Famous Quotes

Here are memorable quotes made by five Americans at the time the colonies were struggling for independence from Great Britain. On the lines below each, write what you think the quote means.

1. "We must all hang together, or assuredly we shall all hang separately."

   (Benjamin Franklin, at the signing of the Declaration of Independence, July 4, 1776)

   _____

   _____

2. "These are the times that try men's souls."

   (Thomas Paine on December 23, 1776, prior to the Battle of Trenton)

   _____

   _____

3. "The happiness of society is the end [purpose] of government."

   (John Adams, in *Thoughts on Government,* 1776)

   _____

   _____

4. "I know not what course others may take, but as for me, give me liberty or give me death!"

   (Patrick Henry, in a speech at the Virginia Convention, March 23, 1775)

   _____

   _____

5. "It is like destroying our house in winter . . . before we have got another shelter."

   (John Dickinson of Pennsylvania, one of the members of Congress who refused to sign the Declaration of Independence)

   _____

   _____

Everyday Life: Revolutionary War copyright © Good Year Books.

Name _____ Date _____

Write a Letter

Imagine you are a Loyalist living in New York at the time the Declaration of Independence was signed. Write a letter to a friend in Great Britain expressing your views on the action taken by the colonies.

Date _____

Dear _____,

_____

_____

_____

_____

_____

_____

_____

_____

_____

_____

_____

_____

_____

_____

_____

_____

Sincerely,

_____

Name _____ Date _____

Draw a Cartoon

Imagine you are a Patriot living in Pennsylvania at the time the Declaration of Independence was signed. Draw a political cartoon illustrating your support of the document. Be sure to give your cartoon a caption.

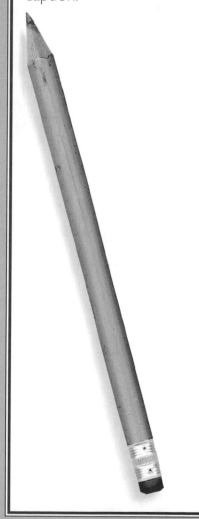

Name _____ Date _____

Answer Questions About the Declaration of Independence

Answer the following nine questions pertaining to the Declaration of Independence. Refer to your textbook or an encyclopedia if you need help.

1. In what year was the Declaration of Independence signed?

   _____

2. What famous American wrote the Declaration?

   _____

3. According to the Declaration, where does the government get its power to rule? _____

   _____

4. What three inalienable rights (rights that cannot be taken away) does the Declaration state that all people are born with? _____

   _____

5. What does the Declaration of Independence say people have the right to do if their government tries to deprive them of the above rights? _____

   _____

6. In your opinion, what does the Declaration mean when it states that "all men are created equal"? What is really meant by "equality"? Is equality in all matters possible, or even desirable? _____

   _____

7. Had you been a member of the Second Continental Congress, would you have put your life on the line by signing the Declaration of Independence? Why or why not?

   _____

   _____

CHAPTER 7

George Washington

Did you know that George Washington was the only president who was ever elected unanimously? Yes, not a single vote was cast against him! How many politicians can make that claim?

And did you know that he never smiled for portraits because his false teeth hurt him so much? You'd probably never smile either if you had false teeth made of wood!

Did you also know that George Washington wore a size 13 shoe, something almost unheard of in his time? Or that one of his favorite childhood activities was copying rules of behavior in a notebook, one of which read "Cleanse not your teeth with the tablecloth"? Or that he never chopped down his father's cherry tree and then confessed because he "could not tell a lie"?

Anecdotes (interesting little stories) about George Washington could fill a book. The same is true of all historical figures, or, for that matter, people in general. Some anecdotes about famous people of the past are true, but many are no more than legends. Parson (pastor) Mason Weems, for example, invented the story of the cherry tree in 1806 in the fifth edition of a biography he wrote on Washington. Weems was true to the tradition of early writers who attempted to make the Founding Fathers of our country perfect and above reproach (criticism). More recent biographies of Washington show that he had faults and weaknesses like everyone else. In other words, he was human.

George Washington may not have been perfect, as some writers would have us believe, but there is no doubt that he was dedicated to his country. After serving as Commander-in-Chief of the Continental Army and leading the colonies to victory over the British, he returned to public life to serve two terms as president. He could have served a third had he been so inclined, but Washington felt that two terms were enough for any president. His refusal to seek a third term set a precedent that remained constant until Franklin Delano Roosevelt sought and won third and fourth terms in 1940 and 1944. (Roosevelt died in 1945, one year into his fourth term. In 1951, the Twenty-

George Washington, Revolutionary War hero and our nation's first President. From an oil painting by Thomas Sully in 1820.

Everyday Life: Revolutionary War copyright © Good Year Books.

second Amendment officially limited the time a president can serve to two consecutive terms.)

George Washington began his career in 1749 as a surveyor. As you probably know, a surveyor is a person who measures land and lays out boundary lines. Not yet 17 years of age, the young Virginian was hired by Lord William Fairfax, an English nobleman, to survey land he owned across the Blue Ridge Mountains. Fairfax's holdings were spread throughout the colony of Virginia, which was considerably larger than the state of Virginia is today. Virginia at that time extended from what is now Pennsylvania in the North to present-day South Carolina in the South. The East-West boundaries of the colony were even more imposing. They began at the Atlantic Ocean and extended indefinitely to the West.

An early map of the Virginia colony, dating from 1612.

Lord Fairfax was so pleased with Washington's work that he helped him secure the position of public surveyor in Virginia. For three years, young George traveled about Virginia surveying the land. The colony paid him 100 pounds a year for his services. One hundred pounds at the time was equal to about $500. Because of his earnings, George, at the age of 20, considered himself quite well-off.

The next step in Washington's career occurred in 1753. Robert Dinwiddie, the royal governor of Virginia, chose him to lead a small party of men on a journey into the Ohio Valley. Washington's mission was to tell the French there that they were encroaching on British territory and that they had best leave. Dinwiddie's motive was purely personal. As a member of a colonial enterprise known as the Ohio Company, he was concerned that the French would monopolize the profitable fur trade with the Indians and squeeze the British out.

Washington was only 21 at the time and a major in the Virginia militia. But to Dinwiddie, he was the right man for the job. Setting out with six companions in October 1753, the future first president traveled some 500 miles before he located the French. The French responded politely to his request that they leave, but they refused to budge.

Washington's instructions from Governor Dinwiddie also included that he try to establish friendly relations with the Iroquois Indians of the Ohio region. In this endeavor he also failed. In fact, he was fortunate to get back to Virginia in one piece. Indians shot at him along the way: he once fell into the Allegheny River and almost drowned. The one-month trip home was probably the longest month in Washington's life.

One year later, George Washington was back in the Ohio region with a force of 150 men. He had been promoted to lieutenant-colonel by Governor Dinwiddie and given instructions to drive the French out. Again, however, he failed. His skirmishes with the French resulted in the firing of the first shots in what came to be called the French and Indian War.

After Washington's failed mission in 1754, Great Britain sent General Edward Braddock to America to deal with the French. He made Washington an aide, and once again the young Virginian was off to the wilderness. In a bitter battle at Fort Duquesne (now Pittsburgh) on the Ohio River, Braddock was killed and Washington came close to sharing his fate. The future "father of our country" had two horses shot from under him and received four bullet holes through his coat.

Mrs. Martha (Custis) Washington, George Washington's wife of 40 years. She shared many of his hardships during the trying days of the revolution.

Washington continued to serve throughout most of the war (which the British eventually won), whereupon he left the military to take up the life of a farmer. In 1759, he married Martha Dandridge Custis, a rich widow with two small children. Their combined land holdings made them one of the wealthiest families in Virginia.

George Washington might have been content to remain a gentleman farmer had Great Britain not decided to make the colonies help pay for the cost of the French and Indian War. As tensions gradually increased from 1763 onward, Washington found himself caught up in the tide of events that eventually led to open conflict. In 1774, he was elected as a delegate to the First Continental Congress. The following year, he was chosen again to serve in the Second Continental Congress. Finally, on June 15, 1775, he was honored by his fellow delegates when they named him to command the Continental Army.

Washington considered himself unsuited to lead a nation's army, but he accepted the challenge as his patriotic duty. He refused any salary, only asking that he be reimbursed for any money of his own that he had to spend to cover his expenses.

Everyday Life: Revolutionary War copyright © Good Year Books.

Washington took command of an army sorely lacking in discipline. Recruits refused to salute their officers and sometimes even beat them up. Guards left their posts when they felt so inclined, believing that since they were fighting for liberty they could do as they pleased. Soldiers spent considerable time gambling, drinking, and engaged in horseplay. Their cursing made Washington shudder.

To bring his troops into line, Washington established set punishments for every offense. Fines were levied for minor violations, a prescribed number of lashes for major ones. Later, Washington brought in Baron Friedrich Wilhelm von Steuben of Prussia to help whip his raw recruits into a well-drilled, well-disciplined army.

In spite of never having enough men and supplies at his disposal, Washington eventually led the Continental Army to victory over the British. You will read more about this great patriot, along with some of the major battles of the war, in Chapter 10, "Major Battles."

Space does not permit a detailed study of the leadership and character of George Washington. Nowhere, however, was this better demonstrated than at Valley Forge, Pennsylvania, during the terrible winter of 1777–1778. You are probably familiar with the story. Washington's troops—starving, diseased, and freezing—were impressed by their general's concern for their welfare and by his willingness to share their hardships. Washington even spent freezing nights talking with and trying to cheer up homesick, young recruits standing guard duty in the snow, no shoes on their feet and mere rags on their back.

Such was the character of the man many historians have called the Father of Our Country.

George Washington in his uniform as commander of the Continental Army. From an oil painting by Charles Peale Polk.

Name _____ Date _____

Find Out Facts About Virginia

Virginia, both as a colony and a state, has played a significant role in our nation's history. Many colonial leaders were from Virginia. The state can also boast of eight presidents who were born there.

How much do you know about Virginia? Here are questions dealing with its history, geographic location, and some of its important citizens. Try to answer as many questions as you can on your own before referring to an encyclopedia or some other source.

1. The first permanent English colony in America was founded in 1607 at _____, Virginia.

2. List any three Virginians from colonial times who played important roles in America's becoming independent of Great Britain. _____   _____
_____

3. The capital of the state of Virginia is _____.

4. Two states border Virginia to the south. They are _____ and _____.

5. Virginia is bordered on the west by the states of _____ and _____.

6. Virginia's three largest cities are _____, _____, and _____.

7. List the names of the eight presidents who were born in Virginia.

_____   _____

_____   _____

_____   _____

_____   _____

Name _____ Date _____

Draw Conclusions from What You Have Read

An important part of reading comprehension is studying facts that are presented and then making logical guesses as to their meaning.

Read each of the following statements and then draw your own conclusions to answer the questions.

1. Benjamin Franklin once suggested that the Continental Army would be wise to discard its muskets and use bows and arrows instead. What can you conclude from such a statement? Did you think it was well-grounded?

   _____

   _____

   _____

   _____

2. George Washington's troops suffered terribly at Valley Forge during the winter of 1777–1778. What can you conclude from the following situations?

   a. Sentries stood guard duty with their feet in their hats.

   _____

   b. Food and supplies were plentiful in Pennsylvania, yet soldiers died of starvation and exposure.

   _____

   c. Loyal soldiers often deserted upon receiving letters from home.

   _____

3. What can you conclude from the following statement taken from Washington's Farewell Address upon finishing his second term as president? "It is our true policy to steer clear of permanent alliances with any portion of the foreign world."

   _____

   _____

   _____

Name _____ Date _____

Solve Some Word Problems

Here are several word problems having to do with events covered in Chapter 7. Solve each in the space provided, and write its correct answer on the appropriate line.

1. General Braddock's British army, because it had to cut down trees all along the way, covered only about 3.5 miles a day in its 110-mile march from Virginia to Fort Duquesne in 1755. In round numbers, how may days did it take the army to reach its destination?

_____ days

2. Washington encamped at Valley Forge in the winter of 1777–1778 with an army of 11,000 men. If 3,000 died from cold, hunger, and disease, and 1,100 went over to the British, how many men did Washington have left?

_____ men

What percent of Washington's army went over to the British?

_____ percent

What percent died?

_____ percent

Name _____ Date _____

Solve a Washington Crossword

Across

4. General _____ Braddock

7. Fort Duquesne today

11. George Washington's wife

12. French and _____ war

13. _____ Forge

14. First Continental _____

Down

1. _____ Duquesne

2. Washington's home state

3. Parson _____

5. Washington to General Braddock

6. Von Steuben's country

8. Number of terms Washington served as President

9. _____ von Steuben

10. Washington's first job

Other Heroes

Much has been written about such American heroes as George Washington, Thomas Jefferson, and Patrick Henry. Just as well known are Thomas Paine, Benjamin Franklin, Paul Revere, and a host of others.

But not all heroes of the American Revolution have been glorified in literature and song. Some, such as Baron von Steuben and the Marquis de Lafayette, were not even Americans. And many others fall into the category of "unsung" heroes. These are Americans who have not been honored to any great degree, but whose contributions were nonetheless important to the cause of liberty.

One unsung hero was Sergeant Ezra Lee. He had the distinction of carrying out the first submarine attack in history. You might ask: "Come on now—submarines in the Revolutionary War? Surely you jest! At a time when even the muskets used in battle were not very reliable, do you expect me to believe they had submarines?"

Yes! Well, one submarine, that is. And it looked more like a top or a coconut than a submarine. Invented by David Bushnell of Connecticut, the *Turtle*, as the strange-looking craft was called, was made of oak and stood upright instead of flat in the water. While on the surface, it bobbed like a cork and was difficult to handle. But it was a submarine.

David Bushnell's *Turtle,* the world's first submarine. It failed in its attempt to sink a British ship in New York Harbor early in the war.

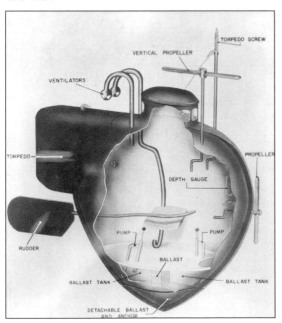

The *Turtle* was a one-man sub powered by hand-cranked propellers. It was equipped with two augers or drills designed to plant a time bomb into the bottom of a ship. Like all other gadgets on the *Turtle*, the augers were cranked by hand. Diagrams of the vessel even show its operator using his feet and elbows to maneuver the craft.

The "driver" of the *Turtle* was Sergeant Ezra Lee, who was referred to above. About two months after the signing of the Declaration of Independence, Lee submerged in New York Harbor and propelled his way to the British ship the HMS *Eagle* off Governors Island. Having reached his target, he proceeded to start drilling into the ship's hull. He drilled, and he drilled, and he drilled some more.

But his efforts were fruitless. Because the hulls of British ships were covered with copper plates to protect them from wood-eating worms, Lee could not penetrate the metal to implant his bomb. Frustrated, he had no choice but to retreat and release the bomb—just before it exploded. Lee was unharmed but the *Turtle* almost sank. Although he had failed in his mission, Lee's attack frightened the British enough to make them move the *Eagle* to a safer harbor.

A hero better known to readers is Nathan Hale. Hale was a young Connecticut schoolteacher who became an officer in the Continental army in 1776. When George Washington asked for a volunteer to go behind enemy lines on Long Island and gather information on British positions and troop movements, the 21-year-old Hale accepted the challenge. The mission turned out to be his first and only as a spy.

Nathan Hale awaiting his execution on the morning of September 13, 1776. He was hanged without benefit of a trial.

Hale landed on Long Island on September 12, 1776. Dressed in civilian clothes, he posed as a Dutch schoolteacher roaming the countryside in search of a job. His cover worked well, and no one suspected he was really an officer in the Continental Army. Moving about freely, he made notes and drawings of everything he saw and hid the papers in his shoes. He successfully completed his mission and was on the way back to his own lines when he was captured.

No one knows for sure how the British found out about Hale. Several sources maintain that he was recognized and betrayed by a cousin loyal to the British. In any case, the boat supposedly coming to take him back to safety was occupied by British soldiers. Hale was arrested and taken to the headquarters of General Sir William Howe. There, he was searched, and the notes he had hidden in his shoes found. He had no choice but to confess that he was a spy.

Hale was granted none of the privileges usually accorded a spy. His requests for a Bible and an audience with a minister were denied. He was allowed to write a final letter, but it was mockingly torn up before his eyes prior to his hanging the following morning. He received no trial. He was simply condemned to die on the spot.

On the morning of September 13, 1776, Hale was led to a tree from which hung a noose and against which was propped a ladder. He was instructed to step up the ladder, at which time the noose was tightened around his neck. When asked if he had anything to say, he turned to his executioner and uttered those words for which he is famous: "I only regret that I have but one life to lose for my country." At that, the ladder was removed and Hale died, a true American hero.

Baron Friedrich Wilhelm Ludolf Gerhard Augustin von Steuben (how's that for a name?) was mentioned briefly in Chapter 7. But he deserves a closer look, not only because he was something of a hero but because he was something of a hero with a comic personality. His tendency to make George Washington's troops laugh—whether by design or accident—probably helped sustain them during their stay at Valley Forge.

What most people did not know at the time was that von Steuben was an impostor. He told Benjamin Franklin in Paris that he was a major general of noble birth who had served as an aide to the King of Prussia. As things turned out, he was no baron at all, and he had only risen to the rank of captain in the Prussian army. Franklin saw through his ruse from the start, but he did not care. He knew that von Steuben was an excellent drillmaster, and an excellent drillmaster was what the Continental Army needed at the time. Whether he was a baron or not was of no consequence.

Baron von Steuben, who helped turn Washington's raw colonial troops into an effective fighting force.

Von Steuben was an energetic person with a happy personality and a booming voice. He spoke very little English, his knowledge of the language being limited mainly to curse words. In a mixture of German, French, and English, he drilled the Continental troops, keeping them in stitches much of the time with his antics. The fact that he worked 12 hours a day and was sincerely devoted to his task won him the cooperation and affection of officers and enlisted men (regular soldiers) alike.

After the war, von Steuben chose to stay in America rather than return to Prussia. He became an American citizen and was granted a small pension. The state of New York was so grateful for his services that they granted him 16,000 acres of land in the Mohawk Valley. Steubenville, a city in eastern Ohio, is named for him.

Everyday Life: Revolutionary War copyright © Good Year Books.

Some of America's other lesser-known heroes you have met in previous chapters. Henry Knox literally dragged the guns of Fort Ticonderoga to the hills overlooking Boston, resulting in the British pulling out of the city. Three African-Americans—Crispus Attucks, Peter Salem, and Salem Poor— distinguished themselves early in the revolution. Crispus Attucks, in fact, may have been the first American killed in the fight for freedom when he was shot during the so-called Boston Massacre five years before the revolution even began. Peter Salem and Salem Poor fought bravely at the Battle of Bunker (Breed's) Hill.

Mention has also been made of Molly Pitcher and Mary Corbin, who went with their husbands into battle and gained fame for themselves. But an even lesser-known woman who made a valuable contribution to the war effort was 16-year-old Sybil Ludington. It is with her exploit that we conclude this chapter about other heroes and heroines.

Sybil Ludington was a farm girl who lived in Putnam County in southeastern New York. On the night of April 26, 1777, she volunteered to spread the word that the British had burned the nearby town of Danbury, Connecticut, and were marching west toward the village of Carmel. Her job as courier was to ride through the countryside and inform members of her father's militia to assemble for action.

This bronze statue in Putnam County, New York, commemorates the heroic feat of Sybil Ludington, whose courageous nighttime ride through the countryside alerted residents that the British were advancing on the town of Carmel.

When Sybil Ludington's ride is compared to that of Paul Revere two years earlier, one wonders why Revere is so well known and Sybil virtually unheard of. Whereas Paul Revere rode an estimated 14 miles to warn the people of Lexington and Concord that the British were coming, Sybil Ludington rode a distance of between 30 and 40 miles. She rode all night and into the next morning sitting sidesaddle on an old farm horse. Each time she approached a house or cabin she halted momentarily and pounded on the door with a heavy stick, informing the people inside of the impending danger.

Today there is a life-sized bronze statue of Sybil Ludington in Carmel, New York, near the Connecticut state line. The statue portrays her sitting on her horse, Star, holding the heavy stick she used to arouse the militia of Putnam County that April night so long ago.

Everyday Life: Revolutionary War copyright © Good Year Books.

Name _____ Date _____

Answer Questions About Heroism

Acts of heroism are not always associated with war. Most heroes, in fact, are found in places far removed from the battlefield. There may even be heroes in your own family, school, or neighborhood.

With the above statement in mind, write your best answers to these questions.

1. In your opinion, what personal traits make a person a hero?

   _____

   _____

2. Name any three well-known national or international figures you consider to be heroes. Tell why you think each is deserving of such recognition.

   _____

   _____

   _____

   _____

   _____

3. Who do you know personally that fits the description of a hero? What has he or she done to be thought of as such?

   _____

   _____

   _____

   _____

4. Ask a relative or friend to name one of his or her heroes. Ask why that person was chosen, then write down what you learned.

   _____

   _____

   _____

   _____

Everyday Life: Revolutionary War copyright © Good Year Books.

Name _____ Date _____

Fill In a Venn Diagram

Fill in the Venn diagram to compare the heroics of Sybil Ludington as a courier with those of Paul Revere. Write facts about each in the appropriate place. List features common to both where the circles overlap.

Sybil Ludington

Both

Paul Revere

Name _____ Date _____

Make a Mobile of Revolutionary War Heroes

You have read about many heroes who played a part in America's fight for independence. Some of these heroes were men, others were women. Some made contributions even before the fighting began. Some are well-known to students of history, while others are seldom mentioned in texts and stories.

With a few simple materials, you can make a mobile honoring some of these heroes of American history. You decide which ones to include on your mobile.

Here is What You Will Need:

1. construction paper or small index cards

2. crayons or colored pencils

3. felt-tip pen

4. hole punch

5. string

6. large clothes hanger

7. stiff wire (optional)

Here Is What You Do:

1. Write the name of each hero on the front of a piece of construction paper or index card cut to a size of 2 inches by $3\frac{1}{2}$ inches. Lightly color each card to make it more attractive.

2. On the back of each card, write facts about that particular hero: what he or she did, why that person is remembered, and so on.

3. Punch a hole at the top of each card.

4. Insert and tie a piece of string through the hole at the top of each card. Make your pieces of string different lengths.

5. Attach cards to the bottom of the clothes hanger.

6. Make a sign reading "Revolutionary War Heroes" and attach it to the top of the hanger.

To make a more detailed mobile, cut pieces of stiff wire in lengths of about 6 inches. Slightly bend each in the middle to give it a rainbow shape. Attach a card to each end of the wire strips. Tie different lengths of string to the middle of the pieces of wire and then hang the strips from the bottom of the clothes hanger.

Name _____ Date _____

Create a Dialogue

You learned in Chapter 8 about Sergeant Ezra Lee's failed attempt to sink a British ship while operating the *Turtle*. On the lines provided, create a dialogue that might have taken place after the attack between Sergeant Lee and David Bushnell, the *Turtle*'s creator.

_____
_____
_____
_____
_____
_____
_____
_____
_____
_____
_____
_____
_____
_____
_____
_____
_____
_____
_____
_____
_____
_____
_____

CHAPTER 9

The Home Front

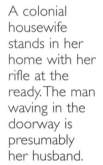

Every war has its home front. The Revolutionary War was no different. The home front consists of the efforts and contributions made by civilians to the cause of victory. It involves the work of men who are either too old to fight or who are exempt (excused) from military duty for some reason. It involves the dedication of women who do everything from sewing clothes and making bandages to offering their services as spies. And it involves the bravery and efforts of children who often perform acts and deeds far beyond their years.

The home front during the American Revolution started even before the first shots were fired. A group of young girls calling themselves the Daughters of Liberty vowed never to marry any man who bought English goods. How about that for a unique way to keep bachelors on the patriot side? History does not say how effective the Daughters' decision was or how many of its members were true to its resolution.

In Edenton, North Carolina, another group of women actually signed a declaration taking a stand against the purchase of any product from England. Led by Penelope Barker, 51 women assembled at the home of Elizabeth King in Edenton in October 1774 to discuss the impending (threatening) crisis with Great Britain. All 51 women signed the paper drawn up by Penelope, swearing that they would neither drink British tea nor wear British cloth. They would drink coffee in the place of tea and spin their own cloth to make their clothing.

After the first shots at Lexington and Concord, women on the home front plunged headlong into the war effort. In the absence of their husbands, they ran farms and operated businesses. They sewed clothes for soldiers and made and rolled bandages. They took in boarders to help make ends meet and free their soldier husbands from worry about their welfare. They fed and cared for wounded soldiers and helped make gunpowder and cannonballs. Some, as you have already learned, even fought as soldiers or served as couriers. Others made invaluable contributions as spies. The story of several in this latter group will be told later in this chapter.

A colonial housewife stands in her home with her rifle at the ready. The man waving in the doorway is presumably her husband.

Everyday Life: Revolutionary War copyright © Good Year Books.

Children also did all they could to help. They performed additional chores in the absence of their fathers and older brothers with a minimum of complaints. They accepted the privations of war, ate less, and did without extras and luxuries. Like their mothers, they helped make cartridges and soldiers' bags or baked biscuits for the troops.

Many young boys contributed greatly as unofficial spies. Because of their size, they could hang around British camps or in towns where British troops were quartered and pick up valuable information. An adult doing the same would have immediately been detained and questioned, but a young boy could do so without arousing too much suspicion. Older boys working as waiters in taverns and inns often overheard pieces of conversation about troop movements or where enemy supplies and weapons were stored.

Some Patriot boys served as guides for General Washington's troops. They knew the countryside better than any adult and could lead soldiers to almost any destination. Some even served as guides for the British and purposely caused them to become lost in unknown woods or to get bogged down in a swamp far from where they wanted to be.

Both boys and girls volunteered as couriers during the war. You read about Sybil Ludington in the last chapter. But there were others. Children could deliver or receive messages right under the noses of the British without the latter even suspecting them. They could also distribute anti-British pamphlets that helped boost the morale of the Patriots. Thus, children were used in many ways to spread propaganda and carry messages.

Boys further served the Patriot cause by becoming saboteurs. This meant that they purposely destroyed or damaged things to hinder the enemy's effectiveness in the field. Sometimes they slashed the canvas tops of wagons, letting in rain that ruined foodstuffs and supplies. At other times, they drilled holes in barrels and let the contents slowly ooze or trickle out. These and other methods were widely used to cause the British as much distress as possible.

Sometimes an entire family worked together to aid the Continental Army. One such family was that of Lydia Darragh of Philadelphia, a 52-year-old mother of nine. Although she was a Quaker, and therefore opposed to the war, she supported the Patriot cause. Not the least of her reasons for doing so was that her 22-year-old son Charles was an army lieutenant stationed at Whitemarsh, less than 25 miles from British-held Philadelphia.

In 1777, Lydia was surprised when British General William Howe established his headquarters in a house just across the street. From the start, she kept an eye and ear tuned in that direction. Whenever she saw or heard anything that might be of value to General Washington, she reported it to her husband. Mr. Darragh wrote the information in shorthand on very thin paper and concealed it inside a hollow coat button. Then John, the Darragh's 14-year-old son, smuggled the paper out of town. He delivered the button to his brother Charles, who translated the shorthand message inside of it and sent it on to General Washington.

While many families worked together to harass the British, others were split in their loyalties. Such was the case of the family of wealthy New York merchant Robert Murray. Although Mr. Murray was outspoken in his support of Great Britain, his wife Mary, and daughters, Beulah and Susan, were staunch Patriots. Such a division of loyalty gave Mrs. Murray an opportunity to save one-third of General Washington's army in 1776.

The date was September 15, 1776. General Washington's army was in full retreat after being defeated at the Battle of Long Island. Two-thirds of the army had made it safely back to their encampment, but a third was slowed down because it was transporting the army's supplies and ammunition. It was this part that was in danger of being cut off by British General Howe and 8,000 British troops. In order to do so, however, Howe's army would have to pass by the Murray home in the Belmont section of New York.

Mrs. Mary Murray delays British General Howe long enough to allow General Putnam's Continental troops to escape to safety.

Inasmuch as Robert Murray had planned to invite Howe and his officers into his home for a cooling drink, Mary Murray took advantage of the opportunity and hatched a plan to save the remainder of Washington's army. She instructed her maid to climb to the cupola of their house and keep an eye out for a large cloud of dust. When seen, that would indicate that General Israel Putnam and the part of the army hauling supplies and ammunition was within sight of Belmont. Mary Murray reasoned that if she could delay General Howe's departure long enough, General Putnam and his forces would be well on their way up the Boston Port Road and on to safety.

Everyday Life: Revolutionary War copyright © Good Year Books.

After General Howe had finished his drink and rose to leave, he was talked into staying for lunch. Tables containing food and kegs of beer were set up on the grounds of the mansion for the general's troops. After eating and rising once more to leave, Mary convinced the general to stay a little longer for a glass of a very special wine that her husband had recently imported. The general again agreed. By the time he rose a third time and actually left, the Murray's maid had come down from the cupola and whispered to Mary that General Putnam's army had passed and all was clear.

Many women contributed to the Patriot cause by tending the wounded. One whose name is recorded in history is Ann Clay.

Saratoga Camp

The Generals in America doing nothing, or worse than nothing.

A British political cartoon criticizes General Howe for "sleeping in his tent" and doing nothing to win the war.

Mrs. Clay is remembered for her courage and dedication in caring for the many wounded American soldiers after the Battle of Camden in South Carolina.

How trying must have been the ordeal Ann Clay and other women went through! During the revolution, doctors had no painkillers to relieve the suffering of the wounded, whose screams of agony were enough to shatter the nerves of even the strongest present. The only thing usually at hand to numb pain was whiskey. When a wounded soldier was given enough alcohol to make him drowsy, he was then instructed to "bite the bullet." This term derived from the practice of having the patient bite down on a bullet to keep him from biting off his tongue during the operation. This done, the surgeon proceeded to operate. Often as not this meant removing an arm or leg with a saw, sometimes one borrowed from a carpenter. If the unfortunate soul had a head wound, this was usually "treated" by boring into the skull with a drill to relieve pressure on the brain. Deep wounds to the stomach and the chest could not be treated. Soldiers with these kinds of injuries were often left on the battlefield to die.

The incidents of which you have read are but a few of the ways civilians served their country on the home front. Without the help of such dedicated men, women, and children, the war for independence could not have been won.

Name _____ Date _____

Fill In a Home Front Puzzle

Fill in the statements at the bottom of the page for clues to complete the puzzle about the home front.

_ _ _ _ _ _ **H**

_ _ **O** _ _

_ **M** _ _ _

_ _ _ _ **E** _ _ _ _

_ _ **F** _ _ _ _ _ _ _ _

_ _ **R** _ _ _

_ _ **O** _ _ _ _ _

_ _ **N**

_ _ _ _ **T** _ _ _

1. Lydia _____, Quaker mother who served the cause of the Patriots

2. William _____, British general

3. _____ Murray, who delayed Howe long enough to save part of an army

4. _____ Barker, who drafted a petition other Patriot women signed

5. Spies, people who seek _____ about the enemy

6. General _____ Putnam of the Continental Army

7. A _____, one who delivers messages

8. _____ Clay, who tended the wounded after the Battle of Camden

9. A _____, one who destroys or wrecks enemy supplies and property

Name _____ Date _____

Finish a Story

In Chapter 9, you learned that young boys often harassed the British by carrying out acts of sabotage. With this in mind, complete the story that has been started for you. Lines are provided for you to expand on the story and give it any ending you desire. Continue your story ending on a separate sheet of paper.

Caleb and Johnny did not make a sound as they hid behind a clump of bushes and watched the British supply train that had halted for a rest. Each boy was only 14, and each knew he would be in for a good thrashing if his parents knew of his whereabouts at that moment.

"We'd best hurry," said Caleb. "If I'm not home within the hour, Pa will drag me out to the woodshed for a good whipping."

"Same here," whispered Johnny. "Do you think that Lobsterback sentry is asleep?"

"I think so," answered Caleb. "Let's go!"

The boys left the cover of the bushes and crept toward the last wagon of the supply train. Their plan was to cut the horses' harness, hoping such a move would delay the British for at least an hour or so. Any act of sabotage, no matter how small, would aid the patriot cause.

The distance from the bushes to the last wagon was only 20 feet. Caleb and Johnny covered the first 15 without incident, but just as they were negotiating the last five, Caleb stepped on a twig that snapped with the sound of a rifle shot. The sentry woke with a start, noticed the boys, and raised his musket.

_____
_____
_____
_____
_____
_____
_____
_____
_____
_____
_____

Name _____ Date _____

Write a Newspaper Article

Pretend you are a reporter for a New York newspaper in the years following the Revolutionary War. Write an article for your paper about how on September 15, 1776, Mary Murray delayed General Howe long enough to save part of Washington's army.

⭐⭐⭐⭐⭐⭐⭐⭐⭐⭐⭐⭐⭐⭐⭐⭐⭐⭐

First, think of three possible titles for your article.

1. _____

2. _____

3. _____

Now write your article, being sure to include answers to the *Who? What? When? Where?* and *Why?* questions as you did in Chapter 2.

_____
_____
_____
_____
_____
_____
_____
_____
_____
_____
_____
_____
_____
_____
_____
_____
_____
_____
_____
_____

Name _____ Date _____

Distinguish Between Fact and Opinion

In Chapter 1, you completed an activity in which you identified statements as either fact or opinion. Below is a similar exercise containing statements related to the material you read in Chapter 9. On the blank line to the left of each, write **F** if you think the statement is a fact. Write **O** if you think it is an opinion.

As you read the sentences, keep in mind that a fact is a statement that can be proven.

_____ 1. People during the time of the Revolutionary War were more patriotic than Americans today.

_____ 2. Men, women, and children on the home front play an important role during wartime.

_____ 3. Children today are less interested in the affairs of their country than boys and girls were years ago.

_____ 4. Some American families found themselves divided in their loyalties when the Revolutionary War broke out.

_____ 5. The women who signed Penelope Barker's declaration in 1774 took a firm stand against the purchase of British goods.

_____ 6. The use of children as spies during the Revolutionary War was a blatant (obvious) example of child abuse.

_____ 7. Lydia Darragh violated her Quaker beliefs when she spied on the British and passed information on to General Washington.

_____ 8. The only painkiller available to surgeons during the Revolutionary War was alcoholic liquor.

_____ 9. Ann Clay was the most courageous of all the women who volunteered their services during the Revolutionary War.

_____ 10. The Continental Army could not have defeated the British without the help of civilians on the home front.

_____ 11. Some women served as couriers during the Revolutionary War.

_____ 12. The Revolutionary War would have lasted years longer were it not for the contributions of people on the home front.

CHAPTER 10

Major Battles

It is one thing for a nation to declare its independence. It is quite another, however, to secure that independence through a show of strength and solidarity.

The Americans, to be sure, had scored some early victories against their foe. They had driven the British back at Concord and, one year later, forced them to evacuate Boston. But a few days after the Declaration of Independence was signed, a British fleet carrying thousands of soldiers sailed into New York Harbor. Their objective was to seize the harbor and use it as a place to receive war supplies from England.

Washington retreats at Long Island after suffering a disastrous defeat in August 1776.

When General Washington learned of the British move, he sent his army southward from Boston to confront them. The resulting Battle of Long Island proved disastrous for the Continental Army. On August 27, 1776, its soldiers walked into a trap and were almost wiped out. Had a thick fog not given Washington a chance to retreat into Pennsylvania, the American Revolution might have ended then and there.

The Battle of Long Island saw the first appearance of mercenary troops on the side of the British. Coming mostly from the German state of Hesse, the German mercenaries' appearance struck fear in the hearts of everyone who saw them. They wore tall, stiff leather hats that made them look like giants. They braided their hair in long pigtails that they let grow down to their waists. And their faces sported long, curled mustaches that they blackened with boot polish.

The Hessians were fierce fighters. They had to be, for any act of disobedience or cowardice on their part resulted in the cruelest punishment. They may also have fought so fiercely out of anger. Most of the Hessians brought to America did not come of their own free will. They were handcuffed and dragged from farms and shops throughout Hesse. Some were seized as they left church on Sunday and packed off to America. Inasmuch as German princes received payment for each German mercenary they supplied

to the British, they went to any length to shanghai as many as they could.

The reputation of the Hessians as soldiers is one reason why the outcome of Battle of Trenton in New Jersey was so important to American spirit. Having been defeated in New York and with winter upon them, the morale among soldiers of the Continental Army was at a low ebb. Washington needed a victory in a bad way to keep his army from falling apart. The opportunity for such came on Christmas night, 1776.

Fortunately for the Continental Army, Europeans didn't like to fight in cold weather. When the snows began to fall, General Howe sent his army into winter quarters in New York. He left a contingent (group) of some 1,200 Hessians encamped at Trenton on the New Jersey side of the Delaware River. Across the river on the Pennsylvania side were about 2,400 of Washington's troops. The task assigned to the Hessians was to prevent Washington from leaving his winter quarters and crossing over into New Jersey.

George Washington conceived a brilliant idea he hoped would result in an American victory. He knew the Germans across the river would be celebrating Christmas in a big way. He knew they would be drunk and not expecting an attack by the Americans. Thinking this way, Washington got his men ready to cross the icy Delaware on the night of the 25th. They would cross in boats manned by a group of Massachusetts fishermen. If all went well, the Hessians would be taken by complete surprise.

Emanuel Leutze's famous oil painting of Washington crossing the Delaware, which is rife with errors. Washington did not stand in the boat during the crossing and the Americans had not yet adopted a flag.

All did go as expected. After a two-hour fight, 22 Hessians were killed and 92 wounded. Exactly 948 were taken prisoner. Washington did not lose a single soldier, and only two were wounded. It was a great victory for the Continental Army at a time when it was needed the most. The Hessians taken prisoner and boated across the Delaware to New Jersey expressed surprise in letters home that they were not eaten, as their superiors had told them they would be if captured.

Washington followed up his victory at Trenton with another at Princeton one week later. The victory at Princeton turned up a British supply dump containing large quantities of flour, tents, blankets, and shoes. With added

provisions and two victories to raise its spirits, the Continental Army was prepared to continue the fight.

The year 1777 was a decisive one in the American Revolution. After defeats at Brandywine and Germantown (in Pennsylvania) in September and early October, the patriots scored a victory in New York that changed the course of the war. That victory occurred at Saratoga on October 17.

In the summer of 1777, the British devised a plan they thought would cut New England off from the rest of the colonies and end the war. It called for three armies to close in on the Americans at Albany, New York. One army, under General John Burgoyne, was to move south out of Canada. A second, under General Howe, was to move north from New York City. A third army, under a Colonel Barry St. Leger, was to arrive from the west.

The British plan did not work out. Howe and St. Leger got involved in battles along the way, leaving Burgoyne vastly outnumbered when he arrived at Albany. The result was a smashing American victory at Saratoga, just north of Albany. The British defeat took 6,000 of Great Britain's finest troops out of the war for good.

The American victory at Saratoga proved to be more than just a triumph on the battlefield. It brought France into the war against Great Britain, which meant that French money and French troops would soon arrive in great numbers. Spain and Holland also joined the alliance against the British. On a fall afternoon in New York, the tide of war had turned in favor of the patriots.

Despite the victory at Saratoga and the attaining of valuable allies, the winter of 1777–1778 was a difficult one for the Continental Army. Encamped at Valley Forge, the frigid weather and the scarcity of supplies severely tested the determination and loyalty of Washington's troops. Of 11,000 who settled into winter quarters there, about 3,000 died of hunger, disease, and exposure. Others were weakened by a smallpox epidemic that swept through the camp. But those who survived formed the nucleus of a disciplined army ready to take to the field again when spring came.

After the indecisive Battle of Monmouth was fought in New Jersey in June 1778, the war shifted away from the North. In the West, tough frontiersmen fought a fierce struggle with the British and their Tory and Native American allies. Fighting was centered along the New York frontier and in the area west of the Allegheny Mountains. It was not until 1781 that the patriots had scored enough victories in the West to provide settlements in

Kentucky and Tennessee with a degree of security.

In the meantime, the war was also being fought at sea. The small Continental Navy, aided by hundreds of private vessels, captured or destroyed nearly 200 British ships. The only major sea battle occurred on September 23, 1779. The *Bonhomme Richard*, commanded by John Paul Jones, captured the 44-gun British warship, the *Serapis,* in a three-hour battle off the east coast of England. The battle was of little consequence except that it produced one of the most famous exclamations of the war. Jones, when asked by the British captain in the heat of the battle if he desired to surrender, supposedly replied, "I have not yet begun to fight!"

The *Bonhomme Richard* and the *Serapis* slug it out off the east coast of England on September 23, 1779.

Most of the fighting after 1778 took place in the South. In December, 1778, the British captured Savannah, Georgia. In May 1780, they took Charleston, South Carolina. Three months later, they inflicted a costly defeat on the Americans at the Battle of Camden.

Patriot losses in Georgia and South Carolina were discouraging to the patriots. But the hit-and-run tactics employed (used) by guerrilla fighters such as Francis Marion kept hopes for victory alive. Marion was a planter whose forces were too small to fight the British in the open. So he and other guerrilla leaders engaged in a series of surprise attacks on the enemy, retreating afterward to the safety of secret bases. The British spent a lot of time and effort chasing Marion, whose escapes into the swamp earned him the nickname "The Swamp Fox."

The harassing activities of the guerrillas kept the British army under General Charles Cornwallis off balance. So too did an American victory at King's Mountain, South Carolina, on October 7, 1780. When American General Daniel Morgan defeated the British at Cowpens, South Carolina, the following January, Cornwallis gave up the state and set up his headquarters at Yorktown, Virginia. It was there that he was trapped and defeated in October 1781, ending the war.

Name _____ Date _____

Write a Letter

Imagine you are a Hessian solider captured by Washington's forces at the Battle of Trenton. Once you realize you will not be cooked and eaten as your superiors have led you to believe, you relax and decide to write a letter to a family member or friend in Germany.

On the lines provided, write the kind of letter you think a typical Hessian might have written after his capture on Christmas night, 1776.

Date _____

Dear _____

_____

_____

_____

_____

_____

_____

_____

_____

_____

_____

_____

_____

_____

_____

_____

_____

_____

_____

_____, (Complimentary close)

_____ (Your signature)

Name _____ Date _____

Make a Shoe Box Diorama

Make a shoe box diorama depicting a scene associated with George Washington and the Continental Army. You might choose to create one of the following:

1. Washington crossing the Delaware on Christmas night, 1776

2. A scene from Valley Forge while the army was encamped there in the winter of 1777–1778. Your scene might depict:

    a. soldiers hovering around a campfire, or

    b. the log cabins built by the soldiers, or

    c. a lone sentry standing duty in the snow, or

    d. Baron von Stueben drilling Washington's troops

Instead, you may want to think of a scene to create yourself.

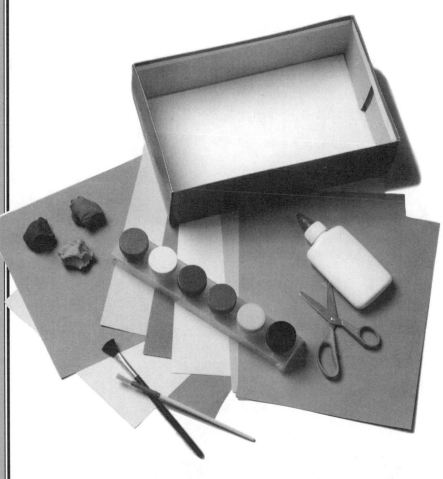

Here are the materials you will need:

1. a shoe box

2. construction paper

3. markers or watercolors and paintbrush

4. glue

5. scissors

6. modeling clay or small figurines

Name _____ Date _____

Arrange in Chronological Order

Listed at right are 16 events that took place during the Revolutionary War. Indicate by number the order in which they occurred.

_____ Battle of Monmouth

_____ Fighting at Lexington and Concord

_____ Battle of Cowpens

_____ John Paul Jones captures the *Serapis*

_____ Battle of Trenton

_____ British surrender at Yorktown

_____ Battle of Long Island

_____ Battle of Saratoga

_____ Patriot defeats at Brandywine and Germantown

_____ Battle of King's Mountain

_____ Washington's troops at Valley Forge in winter

_____ Battle of Princeton

_____ British capture Charleston

_____ Battle of Camden

_____ British capture Savannah

_____ Battle of Bunker (Breed's) Hill

Name _____ Date _____

Use Context Clues to Complete Sentences

Fill in the sentences with the words from the word box.

accustomed	explanations	read	terms
betrayed	introduced	return	things
bravely	needed	served	turn
explain	people	started	war

Every _____ has its heroes and traitors. Sometimes it even has heroes who _____ traitor. The most famous hero-turned-traitor of the Revolutionary War was Benedict Arnold. You may have _____ about him in your history class.

Benedict Arnold _____ out as a patriotic army officer who supported the cause of independence. He fought _____ in several battles, and by the time he was 35 he was a general in the Continental Army.

Several _____ are given as to why Benedict Arnold _____ his country. The most popular holds that he _____ money. His wife, Peggy Shippen, was the daughter of a wealthy Philadelphia banker who was _____ to living lavishly. Arnold could not give her the fancy _____ she wanted on his officer pay, and this may _____ why he went over to the British side. His road to treason was easy because Peggy was a devoted Loyalist who was on friendly _____ with the enemy.

In 1780, Peggy _____ Arnold to Major John André of the British army. Arnold, who at the time was commander of the American fort at West Point, New York, agreed to turn over plans of the fort to the British in _____ for a sizable payment. Their plot, however, failed. André was captured and hanged. Arnold escaped to New York, where he _____ as a brigadier general in the British army. He later fled to England, where he lived out his life, scorned by _____ on both sides of the Atlantic.

CHAPTER 11

The Aftermath

In August 1781, General George Cornwallis brought his British army of 7,000 to Yorktown, Virginia. Yorktown was a small village 25 miles from Jamestown near Chesapeake Bay. Cornwallis reasoned it was an excellent place to receive supplies from the sea. It was. What he could not foresee was that the French navy would sail in from the West Indies and blockade the bay, keeping supplies out and his army in. His setting up camp at Yorktown resulted in his being caught in a trap; two months later he would be defeated and the war would come to an end.

George Washington was in Rhode Island when he heard the news about the French fleet under Admiral Francois Joseph Paul de Grasse. He immediately gave up thoughts of invading New York and hurried south to Virginia as fast as possible. He had an army of 8,000 well-seasoned troops. French General Jean de Rochambeau, who was with him, commanded a French army of 7,800. Together, the combined force of over 15,000 men rushed to trap Cornwallis at Yorktown.

When Washington and Rochambeau reached Yorktown, they were joined by the Marquis de Lafayette, Baron von Steuben, and General Anthony Wayne. (The latter was referred to as "Mad Anthony" because of his reckless courage in battle.) The battle began on September 28, 1781, and continued to October 17. During this three-week period, the British were under siege. A *siege* is when an army is hemmed in on all sides and there is no escape. The French navy prevented Cornwallis from escaping by sea and Washington's combined army of Americans and Frenchmen kept him from getting out by land.

Cornwallis held out for the three-week period, even though he knew he had no chance for victory. After two weeks, Washington brought in 100 heavy cannons and blasted the British for over a week. On October 17, Cornwallis ran up the white flag and the fighting stopped. Surrender negotiations continued for several days. Finally, on October 19, Lord Cornwallis gave his sword to an aide to hand over to General Benjamin Lincoln,

General Washington surveys the battlefield at Yorktown, Virginia. America's victory there ended the Revolutionary War.

who was representing Washington. Except for minor skirmishes that continued for some time, the War of Independence was over.

The British surrender at precisely 2 P.M. on October 19 was not one easily forgotten. Through the ranks of the Americans and the French, who faced each other in rows that stretched for more than a mile, marched the beaten British and Hessian troops. An officer from New Jersey reported that some of the British acted like "little boys who had been whipped at school." Many cried openly. Others bit their lips and pouted when ordered by their officers to lay down their arms. All the while, a British band played a nursery tune popular at the time. Its title was "The World Turned Upside Down." And indeed it was. A powerful European nation had been defeated on the field of battle by an upstart colony.

British troops surrender at Yorktown on October 20, 1781. The French fleet lies anchored in the waters of Chesapeake Bay in the background.

The words to "The World Turned Upside Down" are as follows:

> If buttercups buzzed after the bee;
> If boats were on land, churches on sea;
> If ponies rode men and grass ate cows;
> And cats should be chased to holes by the mouse;
> If the mammas sold their babies to the gypsies for half a crown;
> Summer were spring and the t'other way round;
> Then all the world would be upside down.

What is remarkable about the surrender at Yorktown is that no one realized at the time that the war was over. British General Sir Henry Clinton, Cornwallis' superior, had just arrived from Chesapeake bay with 7,000 reinforcements to rescue the garrison (base) at Yorktown. When he realized that Cornwallis had surrendered, he turned around and sailed back to New York. Washington, for his part, marched his army north. And the French fleet headed back to the West Indies.

Lord North, the British Prime Minister, was one of the few who realized

the significance of Yorktown. When he heard the news, he is supposed to have cried out: "Oh God! It is all over!" King George III wanted to continue the fight, but Parliament refused to spend any more of the British taxpayers' money on a lost cause.

Representatives from Great Britain and the United States met in Paris, France, in April 1782, to draw up peace terms. Benjamin Franklin, John Adams, John Jay, and Henry Laurens represented the United States.

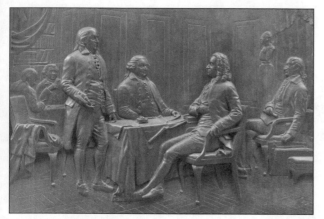

A relief sculpture of Benjamin Franklin signing the Treaty of Paris that officially ended the American Revolution.

Negotiations dragged on for more than a year; what was called the Treaty of Paris was not signed until September 3, 1783.

On November 25, 1783, the British army left New York City. The Continental Army was disbanded, and George Washington happily went home to Mount Vernon. A new nation then began going about the business of governing itself. And what a new nation! The Treaty of Paris more than doubled the area previously occupied by the 13 colonies. The westward boundary of the new United States now stretched to the Mississippi River. Its northern boundary extended to the Great Lakes and its southern borders reached Spanish possessions at the 31st parallel.

The American War of Independence was unique among revolutions. Once over, George Washington did not set himself up as a dictator and no heads rolled. True, some Loyalists were roughed up and a few killed, but nothing existed in America to compare with the guillotine (beheading device) that became symbolic of the French Revolution a few years later.

This is not to say that the new nation brought equality to everyone. Far from it. Free blacks and Native Americans were not allowed to vote, and only those whites who owned property could. Still, America from the start was the most democratic nation in the world. Nearly all Northern states arranged to free their slaves in the years following the revolution, and even Virginia in the South saw 10,000 slaves freed by their masters. (Slavery, of course, would become firmly entrenched there and throughout the South once cotton became king.)

Nowhere was the influence of the American Revolution felt more than in France. Eight years after the British surrender at Yorktown, the French had a revolution of their own. At first, there was little violence and France for a short time was a limited monarchy. After 1792, however, radicals seized control of the government and began a reign of terror that lasted until 1795.

Although the young nation on the other side of the Atlantic Ocean experienced none of the violence that rocked France, Americans still had a rough go of it at first. The problem had to do with the Articles of Confederation. When it was time to decide on a form of government, America's leaders shied away from anything that would concentrate too much power at the national level. More than 150 years of British rule had convinced them that they wanted nothing to do with an all-powerful central government.

So they established a confederation. A confederation is a loose association of almost-independent states. The Confederate States of America some 80 years later was an example of such a government. But at least the Confederate States had a president and an executive branch. The government set up by the Founding Fathers in 1781 had neither. It also did not have a system of national courts. With no way to enforce laws or to interpret them, the federal government established under the Articles of Confederation had little chance of success.

George Washington presides over the convention that approved the Constitution. The Constitution replaced the Articles of Confederation, which had proven ineffective as a plan of government.

There is more. There was a Congress, or national legislature, but it had no power to tax the individual states. It could only ask them for money. To add to the dilemma, each state had its own militia and printed its own money. The federal government also printed money, which meant there were 14 different kinds of money floating around. Anyone traveling, say, from Georgia to South Carolina with a pocket full of Georgia money might have some difficulty buying anything once he or she crossed the state line. It is an understatement to say that confusion reigned in the early days of our country.

For eight years, the United States tried to function under the weak central government established by the Articles of Confederation. Finally, people had had enough. A Constitutional Convention was assembled in Philadelphia, Pennsylvania, in May 1787, to address the problem. Out of this convention came the Constitution of the United States that we live under today.

Name _____ Date _____

Use Your Critical-Thinking Skills

On the lines provided, write your best answers to the following questions.

1. How was the American Revolution different from revolutions that occurred before and after it?

_____

_____

_____

2. How does a revolution differ from a civil war? Are there any similarities between the two?

_____

_____

_____

3. Under what circumstances do you consider revolutions justified?

_____

_____

_____

4. You have no doubt heard of such phrases as the Industrial Revolution or a social or cultural revolution. Can there be a revolution when no fighting occurs? Explain.

_____

_____

5. Bonus. Name any three places in the world today where civil wars are taking place. You are especially clever if you can also explain what all the fighting is about.

_____

_____

Name _____ Date _____

Solve Some Word Problems

Solve the following word problems, and write the correct answers on the blank lines. Space is provided for you to work each problem.

1. On August 14, 1781, Generals Washington and Rochambeau began their 500-mile trip south from Rhode Island to Yorktown, Virginia. If they arrived at Yorktown on September 28, approximately how many miles did they average each day on their march?

_____ miles each day

2. Before others joined the fight at Yorktown, 7,000 of Cornwallis' British troops faced Washington and Rochambeau's combined army of about 15,800. What percent of the total number of soldiers involved were British?

_____ percent

3. Historians estimate that the Revolutionary War cost the colonies about $104 million. By contrast, World War II cost the United States $330 billion. How much more did World War II cost than the Revolutionary War?

$_____ more

Name _____ Date _____

Rewrite a Part of History

One activity at the conclusion of Chapter I asked you to rewrite a part of history based on Great Britain repealing laws to which the colonists objected and even granting the colonies representation in Parliament.

Now you are asked to rewrite a part of history again. This time, suppose Great Britain had won the Revolutionary War. Write how you think the history of America might have turned out differently if the colonies had been defeated.

Name _____ Date _____

Interpret a Bar Graph

The first U.S. census was taken in 1790, nine years after the Battle of Yorktown and the end of the Revolutionary War. As the graph shows, the population of the United States grew steadily after that, more than tripling by 1830.

Use the information from the graph to answer the following questions. (Population figures for each year are rounded to the nearest million.)

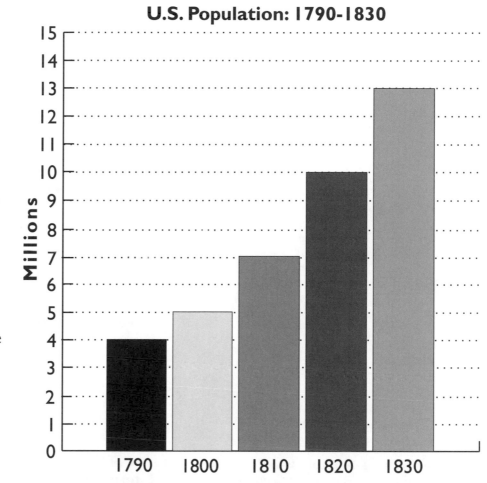

U.S. Population: 1790-1830

Millions

15 14 13 12 11 10 9 8 7 6 5 4 3 2 1 0

1790 1800 1810 1820 1830

1. Between which two 10-year periods did the greatest increases in population occur? _____ and

   _____

2. Which 10-year period showed the least population increase?

   _____

3. How much did the population increase between 1790 and 1830? _____

4. How many times greater was the population in 1820 than in 1800? _____

Answers to Activities

Chapter 1

Name Those Colonies

New England Colonies: Massachusetts, Connecticut, Rhode Island, New Hampshire

Middle Colonies: New York, Pennsylvania, New Jersey, Delaware

Southern Colonies: Virginia, Maryland, North Carolina, South Carolina, Georgia

Chief Products: New England: fishing, shipbuilding, shipping, whaling; Middle: wheat, corn, cattle, fur trading, iron making; Southern: tobacco, rice, indigo, turpentine

Distinguish Between Fact and Opinion

1. O 2. O 3. F 4. F 5. F 6. O
7. O 8. O 9. O 10. F 11. F

Chapter 2

Solve a Resistance Crossword

Across: 1. Adams 3. Port 4. Paul
6. Tea 10. Correspondence
11. Liberty 12. Boston
Down: 1. Act 2. House 5. Attucks
6. Thomas 7. John 8. Jefferson
9. Henry

Chapter 3

Name Those Notable People

1. Patrick Henry 2. Philip Schuyler
3. Richard Henry Lee 4. Stephen Hopkins 5. Button Gwinnett 6. John Hancock 7. Israel Putnam 8. King George III 9. George Washington
10. Benjamin Harrison

Solve Some Convention Math Problems

1a. 40; 43 1b. 43; 37 2. 7; 2 3. 12

Test Your Knowledge of Pennsylvania

1. Harrisburg 2. William Penn 3. Penn's Woods 4. Erie 5. Philadelphia
6. Pittsburgh 7. Amish 8. New York
9. New Jersey and New York 10. Ohio
11. West Virginia, Virginia, Maryland, and Delaware. 12. Phillies; Pirates
13. Eagles; Steelers

Chapter 4

Name Those Synonyms and Antonyms

Possible answers:
1. dawn: sunrise; sunset 2. independence: freedom; dependence 3. concerned: worried; disinterested 4. proceed: progress; withdraw 5. depart: leave; arrive 6. discouraged: disheartened; encouraged 7. responded: answered; ignored 8. disappeared: vanished; appeared 9. excellent: fine; inferior 10. outset: beginning; end 11. powerful: strong; weak 12. succeeded: prospered; failed 13. costly: expensive; cheap 14. included: involved; omitted 15. proud: prideful; ashamed 16. prior: before; after 17. valuable: important; worthless 18. rough: uneven; smooth 19. heavy: weighty; light 20. started: began; ended

Solve Some Battlefield Math Problems

1. 90 2. 1,056; 400 3. 135,000

Make False Statements True

1. Concord 2. John Hancock and Samuel Adams 3. Captain Jonas Parker 4. Eight or nine 5. Colonel William Prescott
6. Boston 7. out of ammunition 8. Ethan Allen 9. New York 10. Champlain
11. Henry Knox 12. Boston

Chapter 5

Answer Questions About a Circle Graph

1. 21,000 2. 31,500 3. 52,500 4. 84,000

Use Context Clues to Complete Sentences

divided; independence; announced; advantages; allies; patriots; fighting; factors; familiar; terrain; lines; tactics; attack; effective; advancing; rows; stronger; dragged

Everyday Life: Revolutionary War copyright © Good Year Books.

Chapter 6

Interpret Some Famous Quotes

Answers will vary but should be similar to the following:

Benjamin Franklin: That unity and oneness of mind was vital for the men who signed the Declaration; Thomas Paine: That the critical position of the Patriots in 1776 would test their spirit and determination; John Adams: That government is designed to serve the people; Patrick Henry: That death was preferable to remaining under British rule; John Dickinson: That it was not wise to break with England before any plan of self-government was finalized

Answer Questions About the Declaration of Independence

1. 1776 2. Thomas Jefferson 3. From the people 4. Life, liberty, and the pursuit of happiness 5. To alter or abolish it 6. Answers will vary 7. Answers will vary.

Chapter 7

Find Out Facts About Virginia

1. Jamestown 2. George Washington, Thomas Jefferson; Richard Henry Lee; John Paul Jones (among others) 3. Richmond 4. Tennessee; North Carolina 5. Kentucky; West Virginia 6. Norfolk; Virginia Beach; Richmond 7. George Washington, Thomas Jefferson, James Madison, James Monroe, William Henry Harrison, John Tyler, Zachary Taylor, Woodrow Wilson

Draw Conclusions from What You Have Read

Answers will vary but should be similar to the following:

1. Muskets were not very accurate 2. a. Many did not have shoes b. Local merchants were hoarding supplies to keep the prices up c. They either became homesick or left to take care of their families 3. That Washington believed the United States should stay out of foreign affairs

Solve Some Word Problems

1. 31 2. 6,900; 10; 27

Solve a Washington Crossword

Across: 4. Edward 7. Pittsburgh 11. Martha 12. Indian 13. Valley 14. Congress

Down: 1. Fort 2. Virginia 3. Weems 5. Aide 6. Prussia 8. Two 9. Baron 10. Surveyor

Chapter 8

Fill In a Venn Diagram

Answers will vary but should be similar to the following:

Sybil Ludington: Younger than Paul Revere: rode more miles; rode an old farm horse

Both: Both set out to warn people that the British were coming; both risked their lives

Paul Revere: Arranged for a signal to indicate whether the British were coming by land or by sea; sought to prevent John Hancock and Samuel Adams from falling into British hands

Chapter 9

Fill In a Home Front Puzzle

1. Darragh 2. Howe 3. Mary 4. Penelope 5. information 6. Israel 7. courier 8. Ann 9. saboteur

Distinguish Between Fact and Opinion

1. O 2. F 3. O 4. F 5. F 6. O 7. O 8. F 9. O 10. O 11. F 12. O

Chapter 10

Arrange in Chronological Order

9, 1, 15, 11, 4, 16, 3, 7, 6, 14, 8, 5, 12, 13, 10, 2

Use Context Clues to Complete Sentences

war; turn; read; started; bravely; explanations; betrayed; needed; accustomed; things; explain; terms; introduced; return; served; people

Chapter 11

Use Your Critical-Thinking Skills

Answers will vary but should be similar to the following:

1. It was not followed by the establishing of a dictatorial government or by a period of bloodshed.
2. In a revolution, people are trying to overthrow an unpopular government and attain their freedom. A civil war involves people fighting among themselves for control. They are similar in that in both there is a desire to set up a particular kind of government.

3. Answers will vary.
4. The word *revolution* means "change." Therefore, any kind of change, whether it involves a war or not, is a revolution.
5. Students might mention Kosovo, Algeria, the Sudan, and Sri Lanka, to name a few.

Solve Some Word Problems

1. 11.1   2. 31   3. 329,896,000,000

Interpret a Bar Graph

1. 1810 to 1820; 1820 to 1830   2. 1790 to 1800   3. 9,000,000   4. 2

Additional Resources

Bliven, Bruce. *The American Revolution.* New York: Random House, 1986.

Clyne, Patricia Edwards. *Patriots in Petticoats.* New York: Dodd, Mead & Company, 1976.

Coggins, Jack. *Boys in the Revolution.* Harrisburg, Pennsylvania: Stackpole Books, 1967.

Davis, Burke. *Black Heroes of the American Revolution.* New York: Harcourt, Brace, Jovanovich, 1976.

Evans, R. E. *The American War of Independence.* Minneapolis: Lerner Publications Company, 1977.

Garrison, Webb. *Sidelights on the American Revolution.* Nashville: Abingdon Press, 1974.

Hakim, Joy. *A History of US: From Colonies to Country.* New York: Oxford University Press, 1993.

Marrin, Albert. *The War for Independence*: The Story of the American Revolution. New York: Atheneum, 1988.

Meltzer, Milton. *The American Revolutionaries: A History in Their Own Words 1750–1800.* New York: Thomas Y. Crowell, 1987.

Morris, Richard B. *The American Revolution.* Minneapolis: Lerner Publications Company, 1985.